Microsoft® Official Academic Course: Supporting Users and Troubleshooting a Microsoft® Windows® XP Operating System (70-271)

Lab Manual

Craig Zacker

PUBLISHED BY
Microsoft Press
A Division of Microsoft Corporation
One Microsoft Way
Redmond, Washington 98052-6399

Library of Congress Control Number 2044116597

Printed and bound in the United States of America.

3 4 5 6 7 8 9   QWT   9 8 7 6 5

Distributed in Canada by H.B. Fenn and Company Ltd.

A CIP catalogue record for this book is available from the British Library.

Microsoft Press books are available through booksellers and distributors worldwide. For further information about international editions, contact your local Microsoft Corporation office or contact Microsoft Press International directly at fax (425) 936-7329. Visit our Web site at www.microsoft.com/learning/. Send comments to *moac@microsoft.com*.

Microsoft, Microsoft Press, Active Directory, Hotmail, NetMeeting, MSN, Outlook, Windows, the Windows logo, Windows Media, and Windows Server are either registered trademarks or trademarks of Microsoft Corporation in the United States and/ or other countries.

The example companies, organizations, products, domain names, e-mail addresses, logos, people, places, and events depicted herein are fictitious. No association with any real company, organization, product, domain name, e-mail address, logo, person, place, or event is intended or should be inferred.

Acquisitions Editor: Lori Oviatt
Project Editor: Laura Sackerman
Project Manager: Susan H. McClung at nSight, Inc.
Technical Editors: Michael Bell, L.J. Zacker, and Steve Hambruch
Copy Editor: Roger LeBlanc
Desktop Production Specialists: Peter Amirault and Mary Beth McDaniel
Proofreaders: Jan Cocker, Tempe Goodhue, and Katie O'Connell
Indexer: James Minkin

SubAssy Part No. X11-02859
Body Part No. X11-02850

CONTENTS

LAB 1

INSTALLING WINDOWS XP PROFESSIONAL EDITION (ATTENDED)

This lab contains the following exercises and activities:

- Exercise 1-1: Performing an Attended Installation
- Exercise 1-2: Setting Up Windows XP Professional Edition
- Lab Review Questions
- Lab Challenge 1-1: Working with BIOS Settings

BEFORE YOU BEGIN

The classroom network consists of student computers divided into two-system lab groups. Throughout the labs in this manual, you will be working with the same two computers, on which you will install, configure, maintain, and troubleshoot Microsoft Windows XP Professional Edition.

To complete this lab, your instructor will provide you with the following:

- A Windows XP Professional Edition installation CD
- A 25-digit product key for Windows XP Professional Edition
- Unique names for your computers, using the format Computer*xx* and Computer*yy*, where *xx* and *yy* are numbers assigned by your instructor. For example, the two computers in your lab group might have names such as Computer01 and Computer02. Throughout this lab manual, the systems will be referenced as Computer*xx* and Computer*yy*.
- A unique workgroup name, using the format Domain*xxyy*, where *xx* and *yy* are the numbers of the computers in your lab group, as assigned by your instructor

SCENARIO

A user has experienced a hard drive failure and, after replacing the drive with a new one, you must reinstall the Windows XP Professional Edition operating system from scratch.

After completing this lab, you will be able to:

■ Perform an attended installation of Windows XP Professional Edition

Estimated lesson time: 100 minutes

EXERCISE 1-1: PERFORMING AN ATTENDED INSTALLATION

Estimated completion time: 60 minutes

In this exercise, you perform a clean Windows XP Professional Edition installation on the first of your lab group computers, which will hereafter be known as Computer*xx*.

1. Turn on your Computer*xx* computer.

   QUESTION   *Why does the system fail to boot?*

2. Insert your Microsoft Windows XP Professional Edition installation CD in the CD-ROM drive.

3. Restart the computer.

4. If necessary, press the spacebar to boot from the CD-ROM drive.

   The text mode portion of the installation begins. The installation program loads a number of files, and after a few minutes the Setup Notification screen appears, informing you that you are installing an evaluation version of Windows XP.

   NOTE   *Installing a Licensed Version*   *If you are not installing an evaluation version of Windows XP, this screen will not appear.*

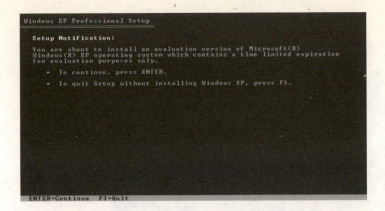

QUESTION   During this initial phase, the setup program gives you three opportunities to interrupt the installation process. What function key must you press for each opportunity, and what services do these interruptions provide?

5. Press ENTER to continue with the installation.

The Welcome To Setup screen appears. From this screen, you can choose to install Windows XP, repair an existing installation, or quit the setup program.

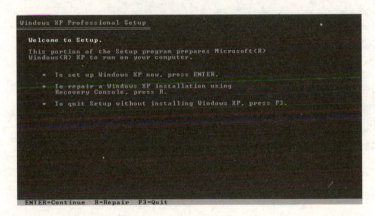

6. Press ENTER to continue with the installation.

The Windows XP Licensing Agreement screen appears.

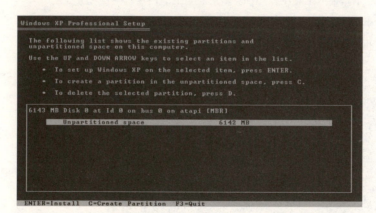

7. Read the license agreement and then press F8 to accept the terms.

A Windows XP Professional Setup screen appears, on which you can manage the partitions on the computer's hard disk and select a partition for the Windows XP installation.

8. Press C to create a partition.

A Windows XP Professional Setup screen appears, on which you can specify the size of the partition you want to create.

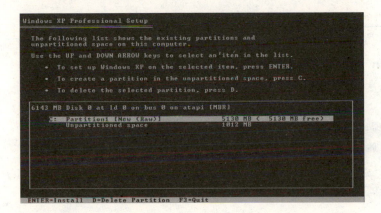

9. Subtract 1000 from the value shown as the maximum size for the new partition, and type the result into the Create Partition Of Size (In MB) field. Then press ENTER.

The partition listing reappears.

10. Select the new C: partition you just created and press ENTER.

A Windows XP Professional Setup screen appears, on which you can format the partition you just created and selected.

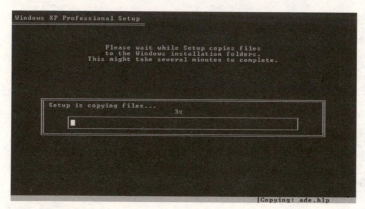

11. Select the Format The Partition Using The NTFS File System (Quick) option and press ENTER.

The setup program formats the partition and begins copying files from the CD to the Windows installation folders.

After the copy process completes, the system restarts.

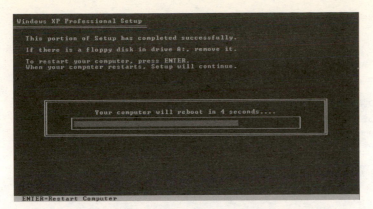

After the computer restarts, the setup program enters the graphical user interface (GUI) mode portion of the installation.

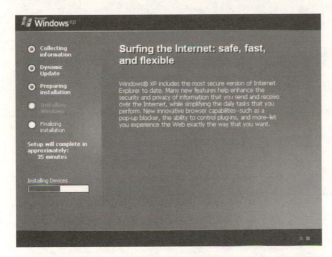

Setup continues the installation for several minutes, and then the Regional And Language Options page appears.

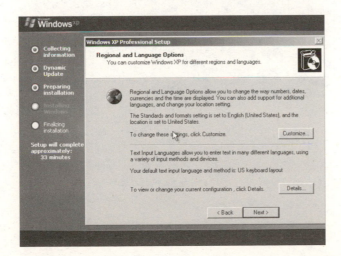

12. Make sure that the settings are correct for your area, and then click Next.

The Personalize Your Software page appears.

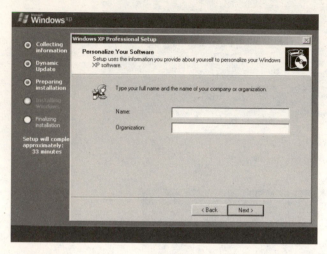

13. Type your name in the Name text box and the name of your school in the Organization text box, and click Next.

The Your Product Key page appears.

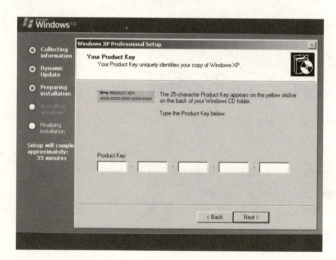

14. Type your 25-digit product key in the fields provided and click Next.

The Computer Name And Administrator Password page appears.

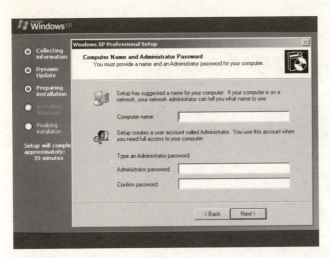

15. In the Computer Name text box, type **COMPUTERxx**, where *xx* is a number supplied by your instructor.

16. In the Administrator Password and Confirm Password text boxes, type **P@ssw0rd**. Then click Next.

The Date And Time Settings page appears.

17. Make sure the Date & Time values shown are correct, and use the Time Zone drop-down list to select your time zone. Then click Next.

18. The setup program begins copying files and installing the Windows XP networking components.

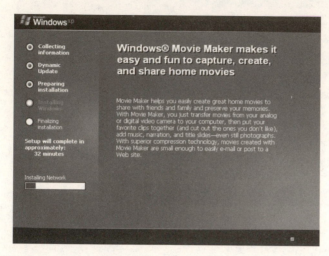

19. To simulate a power interruption, turn the computer off in the midst of the installation process by pressing the power button.

> **NOTE** *Powering Down*   On many computers, you have to press the power button and hold it in for several seconds before the computer shuts off.

20. Wait 30 seconds and turn the computer back on again.

> **QUESTION**   What happens?

Repeat the setup steps, beginning with the GUI mode portion of the installation, until the Networking Settings page appears.

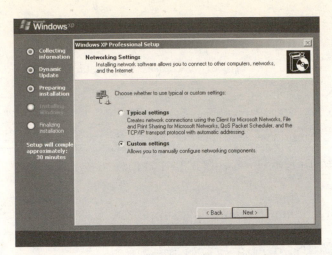

21. Select the Custom Settings option and click Next.

The Networking Components page appears.

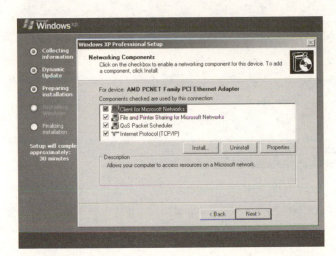

QUESTION   Who is the manufacturer of the network interface adapter installed in the computer?

22. In the Components list, select Internet Protocol (TCP/IP) and click
Properties.

The Internet Protocol (TCP/IP) Properties dialog box appears.

> **QUESTION**   What are the default TCP/IP configuration settings for
> Windows XP Professional Edition?

23. Click OK to close the Internet Protocol (TCP/IP) Properties dialog box.
Then click Next.

The Workgroup Or Computer Domain page appears.

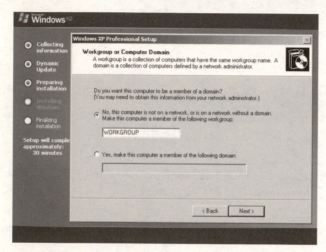

24. Leave the No option selected, and in the text box provided, type
Domainxxyy, where *xx* and *yy* are the numbers assigned to the computers in your lab group by your instructor. Then click Next.

The setup program proceeds to copy files and perform other installation tasks, which can take from 30 minutes or longer, depending on
the capabilities of the computer.

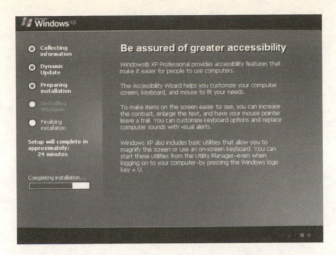

When the installation is completed, the computer restarts and boots into Windows XP Professional Edition.

The Welcome To Microsoft Windows screen appears.

25. Leave the computer turned on for the next exercise.

EXERCISE 1-2: SETTING UP WINDOWS XP PROFESSIONAL EDITION

Estimated completion time: 10 minutes

In this exercise, you complete the setup screens that Windows XP Professional Edition automatically displays after the operating system installation.

1. On the Welcome To Microsoft Windows screen that appears after the operating system installation is completed, click Next.

   If you are installing Windows XP with Service Pack 2, a screen called Help Protect Your PC appears, offering to turn on Automatic Updates. If you are installing an earlier version of Windows XP, this screen does not appear.

2. Select the Not Right Now option and click Next to continue.

   The Will This Computer Connect To The Internet Directly, Or Through A Network? screen appears.

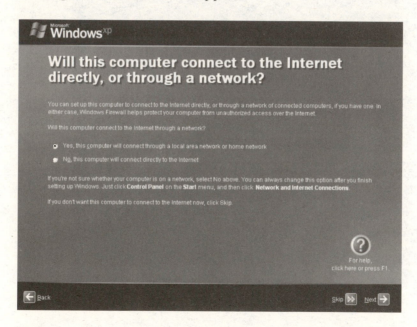

3. Select the Yes option (even if your classroom network does not provide Internet access), and click Next.

> **NOTE**   **Using Windows XP Service Pack 2**   If you are installing Windows XP with Service Pack 2, this screen is called How Will This Computer Connect To The Internet? and has two different options. Select the Local Area Network (LAN) option and click Next. In the Setting Up A High Speed Connection screen, select the Obtain IP Automatically and Obtain DNS Automatically check boxes and click Next.

The Ready To Activate Windows? screen appears.

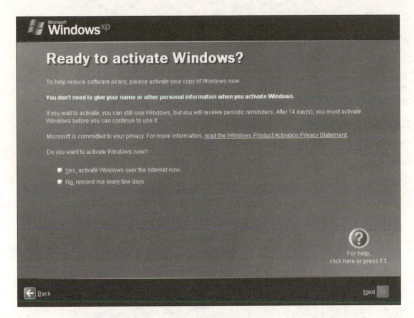

4. Select the No option and click Next.

> **NOTE**   **Activating Windows XP**   If your classroom network provides Internet access, you might be able to activate your copy of Windows XP, but do not proceed with the activation unless your instructor requests that you do so.

The Who Will Use This Computer? screen appears.

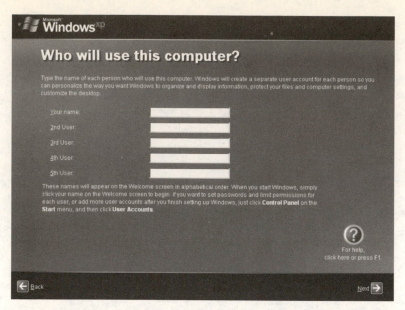

5. Type **Student01** in the Your Name text box and **Student02** in the 2nd User text box. Then click Next.

> **NOTE Creating Users**   This screen creates local user accounts on the computer for the names you supply. By default, these accounts are administrator equivalents. You will learn more about working with local user accounts in Lab 3.

6. The Thank You! screen appears.

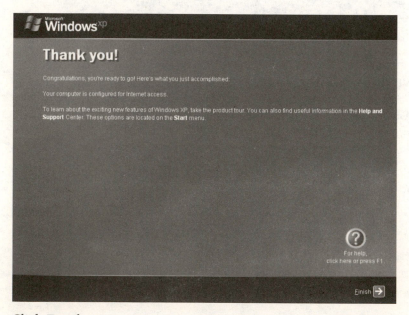

7. Click Finish.

LAB REVIEW QUESTIONS

Estimated completion time: 15 minutes

1. What would happen if you attempted to begin the Windows XP installation process described in Exercise 1-1 with your system BIOS configured with boot devices in the following order:

   a. Hard disk drive

   b. Floppy disk drive

   c. CD-ROM drive

   d. Network interface adapter

2. Which of the following system hardware insufficiencies is most likely to prevent a Windows XP Professional Edition installation from completing?

   a. Insufficient processor speed

   b. Insufficient hard disk space

   c. Insufficient RAM

   d. Missing network interface adapter

3. If the computer on which you plan to install Windows XP Professional Edition already has another Windows operating system on it, how must you modify the installation procedure in Exercise 1-1 to perform an upgrade?

4. List the features that would be unavailable to you if you elected to format the disk partition using the FAT file system instead of NTFS.

LAB CHALLENGE 1-1: WORKING WITH BIOS SETTINGS

Estimated completion time: 15 minutes

In this challenge, you examine the BIOS settings in your computer's setup utility.

1. Turn on your computer, and when the prompt appears, press the key that loads the computer's BIOS setup utility.

   > **NOTE   Loading the BIOS Setup Utility**   Watch the monitor carefully for an indicator telling you what key to press. On many systems, you must press the F2 key, but some computers use F10, DELETE, or another key for this purpose. If you miss the prompt, press CTRL+ALT+DEL to restart the system and try again.

2. The setup utility appears.

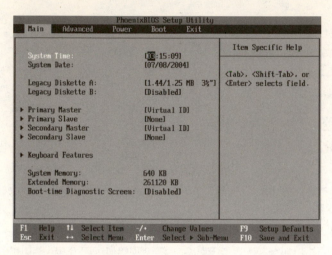

3. Browse through the setup utility's various screens and answer the following questions.

> **QUESTION**   How many hard-disk and CD-ROM (or DVD-ROM) drives are installed in the computer?

> **QUESTION**   How much RAM is installed in the computer?

> **QUESTION**   List the boot devices the computer is configured to use, and list them in the order in which they appear.

4. Exit the setup utility and turn off the computer.

INSTALLING WINDOWS XP PROFESSIONAL EDITION (UNATTENDED)

This lab contains the following exercises and activities:

- Exercise 2-1: Installing Setup Manager

- Exercise 2-2: Using Setup Manager

- Exercise 2-3: Performing an Unattended Installation

- Exercise 2-4: Logging on to Windows XP

- Lab Review Questions

- Lab Challenge 2-1: Debugging an Answer File

BEFORE YOU BEGIN

To complete this lab, your instructor will provide you with the following:

- A Microsoft Windows XP Professional Edition installation CD

- A 25-digit product key for Windows XP Professional Edition

- Unique names for your computers, using the format Computer*xx* and Computer*yy*, where *xx* and *yy* are numbers assigned by your instructor. For example, the two computers in your lab group might have numbers such as Computer01 and Computer02. Throughout this lab manual, the systems will be referenced as Computer*xx* and Computer*yy*.

- A unique workgroup name, using the format Domain*xxyy*, where *xx* and *yy* are the numbers of the computers in your lab group, as assigned by your instructor

- A blank, formatted floppy disk

SCENARIO

You are a new Windows XP support technician for a medium-sized company, and your first assignment is to install Windows XP Professional on a shipment of new PCs the company has just received. You have performed individual Windows XP installations before, but you have only a short time to complete the assignment, so you decide to use answer files to automate the installation process.

After completing this lab, you will be able to:

■ Create an answer file for a Windows XP installation

■ Perform an unattended installation of Windows XP Professional Edition

Estimated lesson time: 110 minutes

EXERCISE 2-1: INSTALLING SETUP MANAGER

Estimated completion time: 10 minutes

In this exercise, you install the Setup Manager from the Windows XP Professional Edition CD so that you can use it to create an answer file in the next exercise.

1. Turn on your Computerxx workstation and log on using the Student01 account.

2. Insert the Windows XP Professional Edition installation CD into the drive.

   The Welcome To Microsoft Windows XP screen appears.

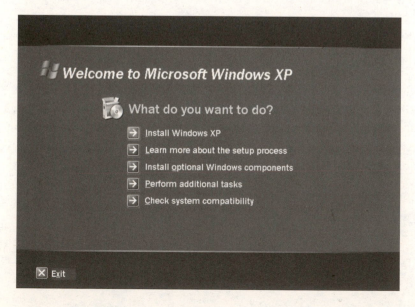

3. Click Perform Additional Tasks.

4. Another Welcome To Microsoft Windows XP screen appears.

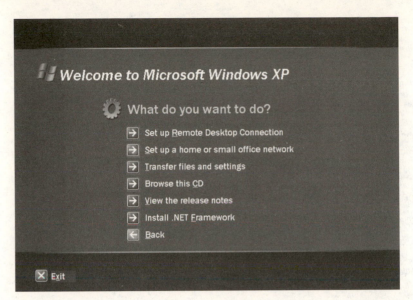

5. Click Browse This CD.

A Windows Explorer window appears, displaying the contents of the CD.

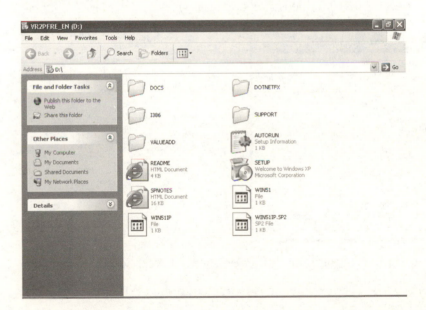

6. Browse to the Support\Tools folder on the CD.

7. Double-click the Deploy cabinet file.

Windows Explorer displays the contents of the cabinet file.

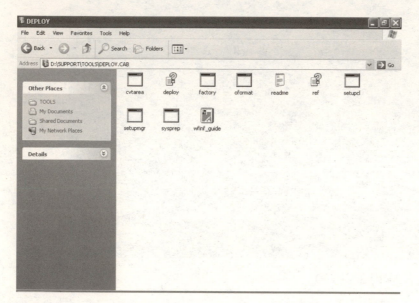

8. Select the Setupmgr file and, from the File menu, select Extract.

A Select A Destination dialog box appears.

9. Browse to the Program Files folder on the C: drive, and click Extract.

The Setup Manager executable is extracted to the C:\Program Files folder.

10. Close the Deploy folder and exit the Welcome To Microsoft Windows XP screen.

EXERCISE 2-2: USING SETUP MANAGER

Estimated completion time: 30 minutes

In this exercise, you use the Setup Manager application to create an answer file, which you will use to perform an unattended Windows XP installation later in this lab.

1. Click Start, point to All Programs, point to Accessories, and click Windows Explorer.

   A Windows Explorer window appears.

2. Browse to the C:\Program Files folder.

   > **QUESTION**   Why does Windows XP hide the contents of the Program Files folder?

3. Click the Show Contents Of This Folder hyperlink.

   The contents of the Program Files folder appears.

4. Double-click the Setupmgr file.

   The Setup Manager application loads, and the Setup Manager Wizard appears.

5. Click Next on the Welcome To Setup Manager page.

The New Or Existing Answer File page appears.

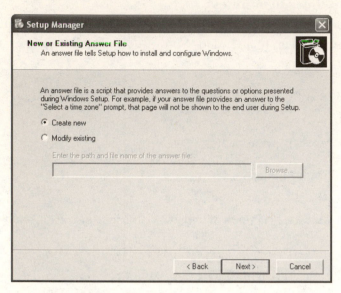

6. Leave the default Create New option selected and click Next.

The Type Of Setup page appears.

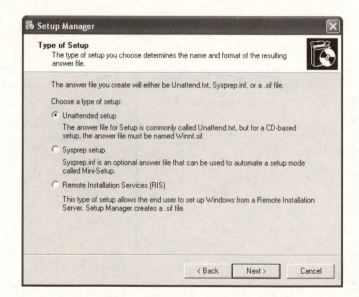

7. Leave the Unattended Setup option selected and click Next.

The Product page appears.

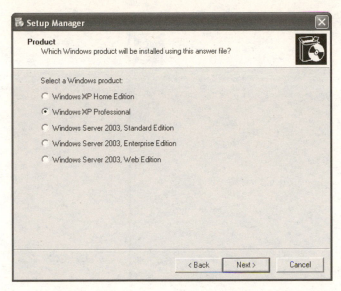

8. Leave the Windows XP Professional option selected and click Next.

The User Interaction page appears.

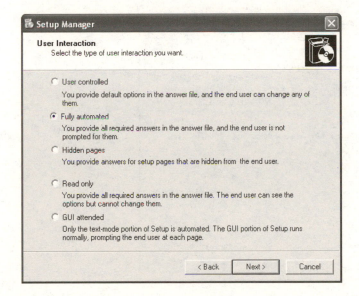

9. Select the Fully Automated option and click Next.

The Distribution Share page appears.

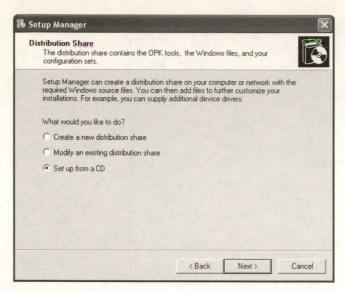

10. Select the Set Up From A CD option and click Next.

The License Agreement page appears.

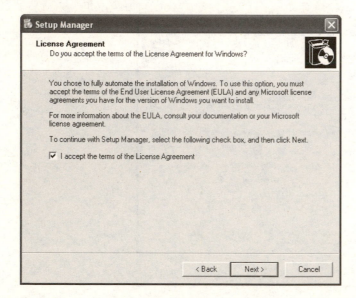

11. Select the I Accept The Terms Of The License Agreement check box and click Next.

The Name And Organization page appears.

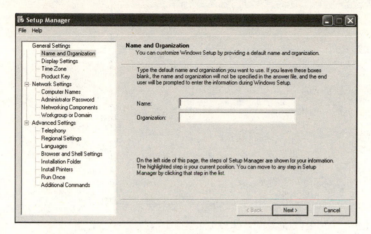

12. Click Next.

QUESTION   What happens?

13. Click OK, and then type your name in the Name text box and the name of your school in the Organization text box. Then click Next.

The Display Settings page appears.

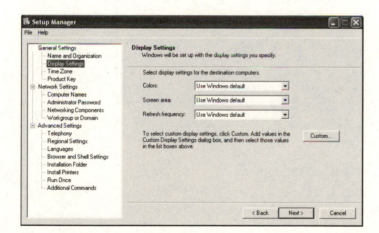

14. Leave the default settings in place and click Next.

The Time Zone page appears.

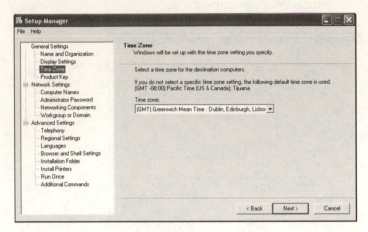

15. Select your time zone in the drop-down list and click Next.

The Product Key page appears.

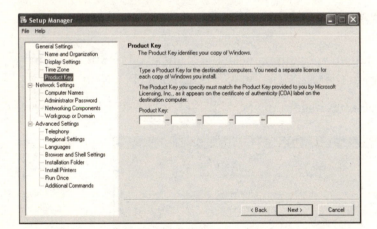

16. Type your 25-digit Windows XP product key in the five text boxes provided and click Next.

The Computer Names page appears.

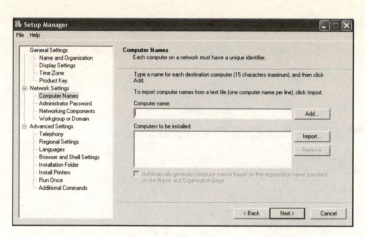

17. Type the name of the second computer in your lab group (Computeryy, where yy is a value assigned by your instructor) in the Computer Name text box and click Add. Then click Next.

> **NOTE** **Performing Multiple Installations with Answer Files**
> Setup Manager enables you to add multiple computer names to the script so that you can use the same answer file to install multiple computers.

The Administrator Password page appears.

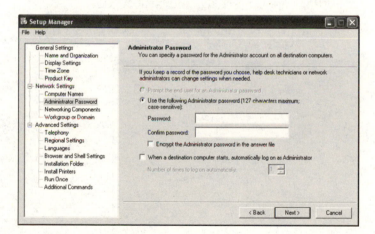

18. Type **P@ssw0rd** in the Password and Confirm Password text boxes.

19. Select the Encrypt The Administrator Password In The Answer File check box and click Next.

The Networking Components page appears.

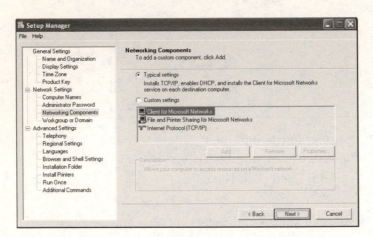

QUESTION   What networking components will Windows XP install by default?

20. Leave the Typical Settings option selected and click Next.

The Workgroup Or Domain page appears.

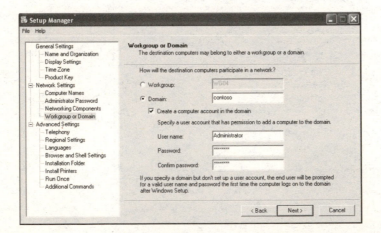

21. Select the Domain option, and type **CONTOSO** in the text box provided.

22. Select the Create A Computer Account In The Domain check box.

23. In the User Name field, type **Administrator**, and in the Password and Confirm Password fields, type **P@ssw0rd** and click Next.

> **NOTE   Creating a Computer Account**   The user name and password you supply on this page are for an account on the domain controller that can create a new computer object in Active Directory. Be sure to verify the name and password with your instructor before you proceed.

The Telephony page appears.

24. Click Next seven times on the remaining pages in the wizard.

> **NOTE   Skipping Advanced Settings**   The Advanced Settings pages in the Setup Manager Wizard contain optional settings that you should not need for your lab computer unless you require regional settings or language support that differs from the defaults. Your instructor will notify you if any additional settings are needed for your answer file.

The Additional Commands page appears.

25. Click Finish.

A Setup Manager dialog box appears, in which you are prompted to specify the location and file name for your new answer file.

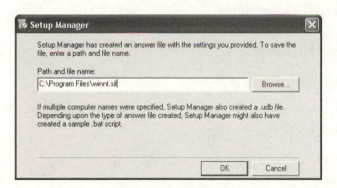

26. In the Path And File Name text box, type **C:\Program Files\winnt.sif** and click OK.

The Completing Setup Manager page appears.

27. Click Cancel to close the Setup Manager Wizard. Close Windows Explorer.

28. Insert the floppy disk supplied by your instructor into your computer's floppy drive, and use Windows Explorer to copy the Winnt.sif file you just created to the root of the disk.

EXERCISE 2-3: PERFORMING AN UNATTENDED INSTALLATION

Estimated completion time: 45 minutes

In this exercise, you perform an unattended Windows XP Professional installation on the second of your lab computers.

1. Turn on your Computeryy workstation.

As in Lab 1, the system fails to start because there is no bootable CD, floppy disk, or hard disk in the computer.

2. Insert your Microsoft Windows XP Professional installation CD in the
    CD-ROM drive.

3. Restart the computer.

4. Press the spacebar to boot from the CD-ROM drive.

5. As soon as you see the words Setup Is Inspecting Your Computer's
    Hardware Configuration, insert the floppy disk containing the
    Winnt.sif file into the floppy drive.

> **NOTE   Accessing a Winnt.sif File on Floppy Disk**   If you don't insert
> the floppy disk fast enough, the system will begin performing a normal
> attended installation. If this happens, restart the computer and try
> again.

Within a few seconds, the floppy drive light will go on as the system
reads the Winnt.sif file from the disk.

6. As soon as the floppy drive light goes out, eject the floppy disk from
    the drive.

    The installation procedure proceeds unattended until the Windows XP
    Professional Setup screen appears. It is on this screen that you must
    create and select the partition for the Windows XP installation.

> **QUESTION**   Why does the installation stop at this point?

7. Press ENTER twice to create a new partition, and format it using the
    NTFS file system.

    The rest of the installation proceeds unattended and uninterrupted.
    After the installation completes, the system restarts.

EXERCISE 2-4: LOGGING ON TO WINDOWS XP

Estimated completion time: 10 minutes

In this exercise, you log on to Computeryy for the first time.

1. On Computeryy, after the Windows XP installation is completed and
    the computer is restarted, the Welcome To Windows dialog box
    appears.

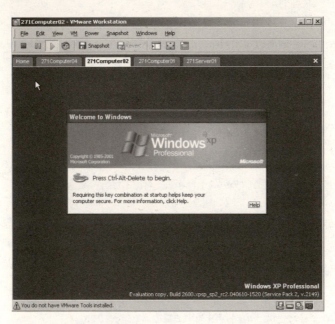

2. Press CTRL+ALT+DEL.

    The Log On To Windows dialog box appears.

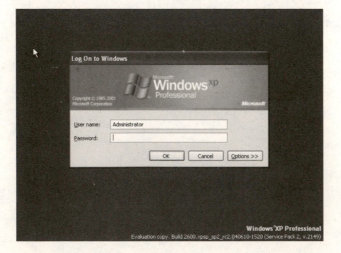

3. Leave Administrator as the default User Name value and, in the Password text box, type **P@ssw0rd**. Then click OK.

> **QUESTION**   What differences do you notice about the behavior of this Windows XP computer, as compared to Computerxx, which you installed in Lab 1.

4. Click Start and select Shut Down.

The Shut Down Windows dialog box appears.

5. Select OK to shut down Windows XP Professional Edition.

LAB REVIEW QUESTIONS

Estimated completion time: 15 minutes

1. During an unattended installation like the one you performed in Exercise 2-3, after the computer restarts for the first time, a message appears stating that an operating system can't be found. What is likely to be the problem, and how should you remedy it?

2. What is the primary advantage of using a distribution share rather than a CD to perform operating system installations?

3. In Exercise 2-3, why is it necessary to eject the disk from the drive during the installation?

4. Why does the Windows XP computer you installed in this lab behave differently than the one you installed in Lab 1?

LAB CHALLENGE 2-1: DEBUGGING AN ANSWER FILE

Estimated completion time: 60 minutes

In Exercise 2-3, your unattended installation was interrupted because the answer file you created expected to find a partition already created on the computer's hard disk. To complete this lab challenge, your task is to modify your answer file to overcome this problem and repeat the installation, this time without any manual intervention.

1. Extract the Ref.chm help file from the \Support\Tools\Deploy cabinet file on the Windows XP Professional installation CD.

2. Look in the Ref.chm file for information on the answer file's [Unattended] section, and locate the command that will enable the installation to proceed completely unattended.

3. Edit the Winnt.sif file on the floppy disk you created in Exercise 2-2 using Notepad, and add the command you found in the help file.

4. Save a copy of your modified answer file with the name ComputeryyLab02-1.sif, where *yy* is the number assigned to the computer by your instructor, for submission at the end of the lab.

5. Repeat the unattended installation procedure you first performed in Exercise 2-3 on your Computeryy workstation.

SUPPORTING LOCAL USERS AND GROUPS

This lab contains the following exercises and activities:

■ Exercise 3-1: Creating a Local User on a Stand-Alone Workstation

■ Exercise 3-2: Changing the Windows XP Workgroup Logon Options

■ Exercise 3-3: Using the Local Users and Groups Snap-In

■ Exercise 3-4: Creating Local Users on a Domain Workstation

■ Exercise 3-5: Working with Built-In Groups

■ Exercise 3-6: Creating Local Groups

■ Lab Review Questions

■ Lab Challenge 3-1: Creating Domain Users

BEFORE YOU BEGIN

To complete this lab, you must have the following:

■ The names (Computerxx and Computeryy) assigned to your computers by your instructor

SCENARIO

You are a new Microsoft Windows XP support technician for Contoso, Ltd., a company with workstations in a variety of environments. Some of the Windows XP Professional computers are members of a workgroup, while others are members of an Active Directory directory service domain. You have been assigned the task of creating user and group accounts for the new employees that the company has recently hired, and assigning them the privileges they need to access various company resources. Because of the differing system configurations, the procedures for creating the users and groups vary.

After completing this lab, you will be able to:

■ Create local user accounts on workgroup and domain computers

■ Create local groups and manage group memberships

Estimated lesson time: 140 minutes

EXERCISE 3-1: CREATING A LOCAL USER ON A STAND-ALONE WORKSTATION

Estimated completion time: 15 minutes

The computers for the users in the Accounting department at Contoso, Ltd., are not members of the corporate domain. The IT director has decided that, for security reasons, these computers should be members of a workgroup, with each computer responsible for its own user authentication and access control. Several of the new hires will be working in the Accounting department, so you must create local user and group accounts on their computers, both for the users themselves and the other personnel who will require access to their files. In this exercise, you create a local user account with the standard User Accounts interface provided in Windows XP Professional Edition.

1. Turn on your Computer*xx* workstation (where *xx* is the number assigned to your computer by your instructor).

2. When the To Begin, Click Your User Name window appears, click the Student01 icon.

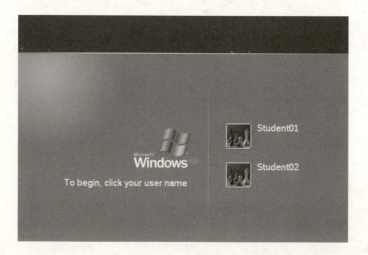

3. Click Start, and then click Control Panel.

The Control Panel window appears.

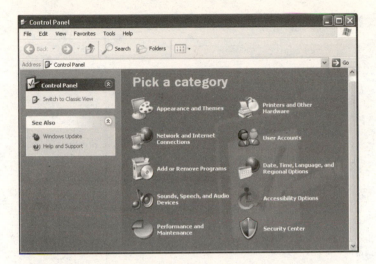

4. Click the User Accounts icon.

The User Accounts window appears.

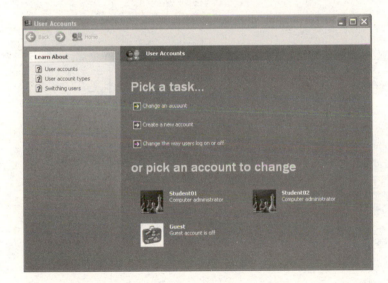

QUESTION What local user accounts are currently listed on the computer?

5. Click Create A New Account.

The Name The New Account page appears.

6. In the Type A Name For The New Account text box, type **JudyL** and click Next.

The Pick An Account Type page appears.

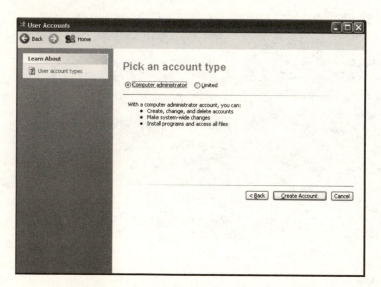

7. Verify that the Computer Administrator option is selected and then click Create Account.

   The User Accounts window reappears, with an icon for the JudyL account you just created added to it.

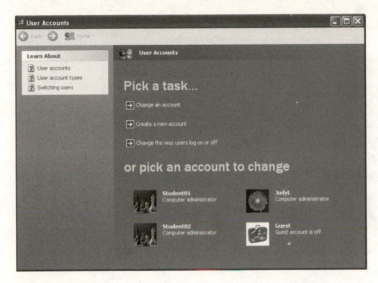

8. Click the JudyL icon.

   The What Do You Want To Change About JudyL's Account? page appears.

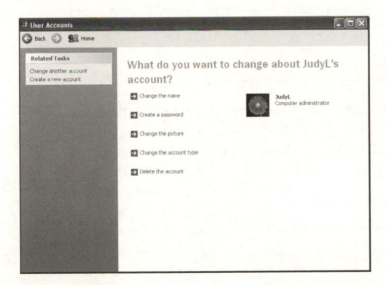

9. Click Create A Password.

The Create A Password For JudyL's Account page appears.

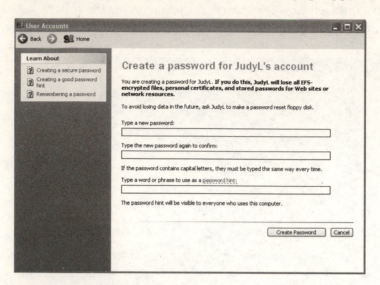

10. In the Type A New Password text box, type **P@ssw0rd**.

11. In the Type The New Password Again To Confirm text box, type **P@ssw0rd**. Then click Create Password.

> **NOTE   Using Passwords**   Leave the Type A Word Or Phrase To Use As A Password Hint text box blank. Providing hints about passwords might be helpful for users, but it also weakens the security of the authentication system.

12. Click Home to return to the User Accounts window.

13. Take a screen shot of the User Accounts window (by pressing ALT+ PRT SCR) and then paste it into a WordPad document named Computer*xx*Lab03-1.rtf (where *xx* is the number assigned to your computer by your instructor) to turn in at the end of the lab.

14. Close all open windows.

15. Click Start, and then click Log Off.

The Log Off Windows dialog box appears.

16. Click Log Off.

    The To Begin, Click Your User Name window appears again.

    > **QUESTION**   What accounts are currently available for logon on this
    > screen?

17. Click the JudyL icon.

18. Type **P@ssw0rd** in the text box provided, and click the right arrow
    button.

19. Click Start, and then click Log Off.

    The Log Off Windows dialog box appears.

20. Click Log Off.

    The To Begin, Click Your User Name window appears yet again.

21. Leave the computer as is for the next exercise.

EXERCISE 3-2: CHANGING THE WINDOWS XP WORKGROUP LOGON OPTIONS

Estimated completion time: 10 minutes

By default, Windows XP Professional, when operating as a member of a workgroup, displays a To Begin, Click Your User Name window when the system
boots, enabling a user to select any of the computer's local accounts when logging
on. This window is a security hazard because it informs potential attackers of the
accounts present on the system. For example, you saw in Exercise 3-1 that the
Student01 account has administrative privileges and is not password protected. If
not for the screen displaying the user accounts, an attacker would not know that
the Student01 account exists and probably would not use it to access the system.
Because of this window, however, simply clicking the Student01 icon gives any
user full access to the computer.

To enhance the security of the workgroup computers, you have decided to
require passwords for all user accounts and require all users to specify their user
names and passwords when logging on. In this exercise, you assign passwords to
the existing computer accounts that are unprotected by passwords, and modify
the system's default logon options.

1. On Computer*xx* (where *xx* is the number assigned to your computer by your instructor), on the To Begin, Click Your User Name window, click the Student01 icon to log on.

2. Open the User Accounts window as you did in Exercise 3-1.

> **QUESTION**   Which user accounts on the computer are not currently password protected?

3. Click the Student01 icon.

   The What Do You Want To Change About Your Account? page appears.

4. Assign the Student01 account a password, using the value **P@ssw0rd**.

   The Do You Want To Make Your Files And Folders Private? page appears.

5. Click No to continue.

6. Use the same process to assign Student02 the **P@ssw0rd** password.

7. Return to the User Accounts window.

8. Click Change The Way Users Log On Or Off.

   The Select Logon And Logoff Options page appears.

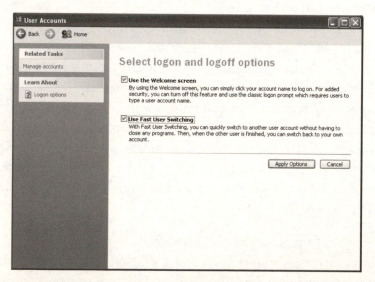

9. Clear the Use The Welcome Screen option. Then click Apply Options.

10. Close the User Accounts window and Control Panel.

11. Log off the computer.

QUESTION   What has changed about the logon process?

12. Log on using the Administrator account and the password **P@ssw0rd**.

> **NOTE   Using the Administrator Account**   In addition to requir-
> ing users to specify their names and password when logging on,
> clearing the Use The Welcome Screen option also makes it possible
> to log on directly using the Administrator account.

13. Leave the computer logged on for the next exercise.

EXERCISE 3-3: USING THE LOCAL USERS AND GROUPS SNAP-IN

Estimated completion time: 20 minutes

You have discovered that while the User Accounts window makes it easy to create accounts for local users, it does not provide access to all the user account properties you need to secure the computer. Therefore, you decide to create the rest of the local accounts for the computer using the Local Users And Groups snap-in for Microsoft Management Console (MMC) instead.

1. On Computer*xx* (where *xx* is the number assigned to your computer by your instructor), open Control Panel and select Performance And Maintenance.

The Performance And Maintenance window appears.

2. Click Administrative Tools.

The Administrative Tools window appears.

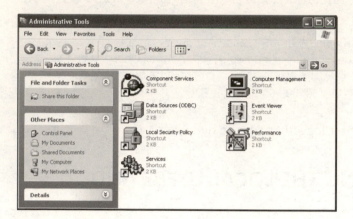

3. Double-click the Computer Management icon.

The Computer Management console appears.

4. In the console tree, expand the Local Users And Groups node and click the Users folder.

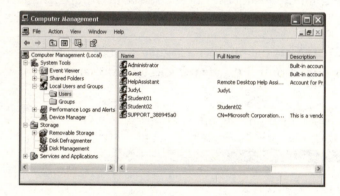

> **QUESTION** What user accounts do you see in the console that you could not see in the User Accounts window in Exercise 3.1?

5. Click the Student01 user account and, from the Action menu, select Properties.

The Student01 Properties dialog box appears.

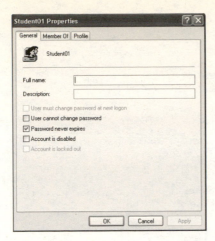

6. On the General tab, select the Account Is Disabled check box and click OK.

> **QUESTION**   What happens to the account in the console?

7. Disable the Student02 account in the same manner.

> **QUESTION**   Why is it practical to disable the Student01 and Student02 accounts now?

8. Open the Properties dialog box for the JudyL account you created in Exercise 3-1.

9. On the General tab, in the Full Name text box, type **Judy Lew**.

10. Clear the Password Never Expires check box, and select the User Must Change Password At Next Logon check box. Then click OK.

> **NOTE   Full Names and Account Names**   Notice that while the full name associated with the account changes to Judy Lew, the actual account name, which the user will specify when logging on, is still JudyL.

11. Click the Users folder and, from the Action menu, select New User.

The New User dialog box appears.

12. In the User Name text box, type **DeborahP**.

13. In the Full Name text box, type **Deborah Poe**.

14. In the Password and Confirm Password text boxes, type **P@ssw0rd**.

15. Leave the User Must Change Password At Next Logon check box selected and click Create. Then click Close.

The DeborahP user account appears in the Users folder.

16. Using the same procedure, password, and settings, create three more user accounts using the information in the following table.

User Name	Full Name
MaxB	Max Benson
CynthiaR	Cynthia Randall
KatieJ	Katie Jordan

17. Take a screen shot of the Computer Management console (by pressing ALT+PRT SCR) displaying the contents of the Users folder, and then paste it into a WordPad document named Computer*xx*Lab03-2.rtf (where *xx* is the number assigned to your computer by your instructor) to turn in at the end of the lab.

18. Close all open windows.

19. Log off the computer.

EXERCISE 3-4: CREATING LOCAL USERS ON A DOMAIN WORKSTATION

Estimated completion time: 20 minutes

Many workstations on the Contoso, Ltd. network are members of a domain called Contoso.com. While in most cases, users log on to domain workstations using domain accounts, certain tasks require a local user account. As a result, the IT director at Contoso has decided that every workstation, whether part of a workgroup or a domain, should have local user accounts for various personnel who might require access to the computer. In this exercise, you create the same local user accounts on your Computer*yy* that you did on Computer*xx* in Exercise 3-3.

1. Turn on Computer*yy*, and log on to the local system as Administrator.

> **NOTE** **Logging On** Make sure the Log On To drop-down list is set to Computer*yy* (This Computer) when you log on. For this exercise, you want to log on to the local computer, not the Contoso domain.

> **QUESTION** How is the process of logging on to this computer different from the newly configured logon process on Computer*xx*?

2. Open Control Panel, and click the User Accounts icon.

The User Accounts dialog box appears.

> **QUESTION**   How is this dialog box different from the User Account window you worked with on Computerxx?

3. Click Add.

The Add New User Wizard appears.

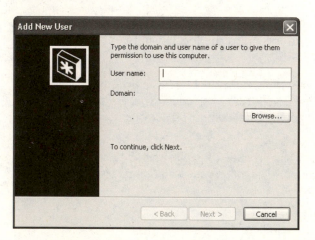

4. In the User Name text box, type **DeborahP** and click Next.

The next page of the wizard appears, prompting you to select the level of access to be granted to the new user account.

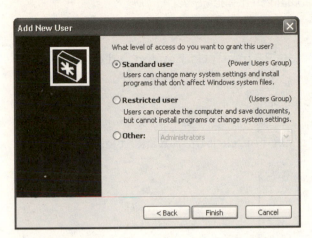

5. Leave the default Standard User option selected, and click Finish.

QUESTION   What happens?

NOTE   **User Accounts and Domains**   The wizard fails to add the user account in this case because the account for DeborahP does not exist in the Contoso.com domain. On a Windows XP workstation that is joined to a domain, the User Accounts dialog box is only able to create local user accounts from existing domain users. To create new local user accounts from scratch, you must use the Local Users And Groups snap-in.

6. Click OK, and then click Cancel to close the Add New User wizard.

7. Click Add to open the Add New User Wizard again.

8. In the User Name text box, type **Studentxx**, where *xx* is the number assigned to your computer.

9. In the Domain text box, type **CONTOSO** and click Next.

> **NOTE** **Using Student Accounts** *Studentxx is a user account in the Contoso.com domain that was created by your instructor during the classroom server installation.*

10. On the next page, select the Restricted User option and click Finish.

> **QUESTION** *What happens?*

11. On the User Accounts dialog box, click the Advanced tab.

12. In the Advanced User Management group box, click Advanced.

The Local Users And Groups console appears.

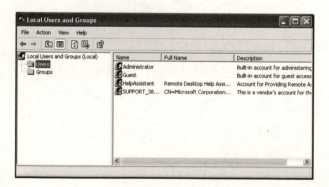

NOTE   Using the Local Users and Groups Snap-In   When you click Advanced, the Local Users And Groups snap-in appears in its own MMC console. The interface is exactly the same as when the snap-in appears as part of the Computer Management console (as you saw in Exercise 3-3).

13. Using the same technique as in Exercise 3-3, create five local user accounts, using the information in the following table.

User Name	Full Name
JudyL	Judy Lew
DeborahP	Deborah Poe
MaxB	Max Benson
CynthiaR	Cynthia Randall
KatieJ	Katie Jordan

For all five accounts you create, use **P@ssw0rd** for the password and leave the User Must Change Password At Next Logon check box selected.

14. Take a screen shot of the Local Users And Groups console displaying the contents of the Users folder (by pressing ALT+PRT SCR), and then paste it into a WordPad document named ComputeryyLab03-3.rtf (where *yy* is the number assigned to your computer by your instructor) to turn in at the end of the lab.

15. Close the Word Pad, Local Users And Groups, and User Accounts windows.

16. Log off the computer.

EXERCISE 3-5: WORKING WITH BUILT-IN GROUPS

Estimated completion time: 20 minutes

When you create local user accounts with the User Accounts interface, Windows XP provides a simple means of assigning privileges to users. When you select options such as Computer Administrator or Limited on a workgroup computer and Standard User or Restricted User on a domain computer, you are actually selecting the group that the new user will be made a member of.

The five users for whom you have created accounts perform the following roles:

- Judy Lew—Primary user of Computerxx
- Deborah Poe—Department Manager
- Max Benson—Primary user of Computeryy
- Cynthia Randall—Department Manager
- Katie Jordan—Administrative Assistant

The IT director of Contoso, Ltd. has decided that the primary user of a computer should be a member of the Users and Power Users groups, department managers should be members of the Users and Administrators groups, and administrative assistants should be members of the Users group only. Primary users should also be members of the Users group on other users' computers. In this exercise, you configure the new user accounts you created in the previous exercises by adding them to the appropriate groups.

1. Log on to Computerxx as Administrator.

2. Open the Computer Management console, and expand the Local Users And Groups node.

3. Click the Groups folder.

> **QUESTION**   What built-in groups are on the computer?

4. Click the Users folder.

5. Open the Properties dialog box for the JudyL user account you created in Exercise 3-1, and click the Member Of tab.

> **QUESTION**   Which group or groups is Judy Lew a member of?

6. Click OK to close the dialog box, open the Properties dialog box for the DeborahP account you created in Exercise 3-3, and click the Member Of tab.

QUESTION   Which group or groups is DeborahP a member of?

7. On the Member Of tab in the DeborahP Properties dialog box, click Add.

   The Select Groups dialog box appears.

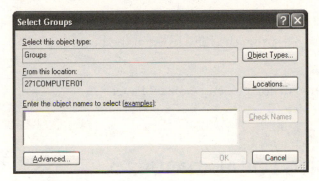

8. In the Enter The Object Names To Select box, type **Administrators** and click OK.

   The Administrators group is added to DeborahP's Member Of list.

9. Click OK to close the DeborahP Properties dialog box.

10. Open the JudyL Properties dialog box again.

11. On the Member Of tab, select the Administrators group and click Remove.

12. Add the Power Users group to JudyL's Member Of list.

13. Click OK to close the JudyL Properties dialog box.

14. Open the Properties dialog boxes for the remaining three users you created in Exercise 3-3, and configure them with the appropriate group memberships, as stated at the beginning of this exercise.

15. Take a screen shot of the Member Of tab in each of the five users' Properties dialog boxes (by pressing ALT+PRT SCR), and paste all of them into a WordPad document named ComputerxxLab03-4.rtf (where *xx* is the number assigned to your computer by your instructor) to turn in at the end of the lab.

16. Close WordPad, the Computer Management console, and the Administrative Tools window.

17. Log off Computerxx.

18. Log on to Computeryy using the local Administrator account.

19. Configure the group memberships for each of the five user accounts you created in Exercise 3-4, using the roles listed at the beginning of this exercise.

20. Close the User Accounts dialog box and Control Panel.

21. Log off Computeryy.

EXERCISE 3-6: CREATING LOCAL GROUPS

Estimated completion time: 10 minutes

Contoso's director of IT has ordered that every workgroup computer have two additional local groups created on it, called ACCOUNTING and BOOKKEEPING. Of the five user accounts you created earlier, the department managers are to be members of the ACCOUNTING group, while the remaining three users are to be members of the BOOKKEEPING group. In this exercise, you create these two groups and add the appropriate users as members.

1. Log on to Computerxx as Administrator.

2. Open the Computer Management console, and expand the Local Users And Groups node.

3. Click the Groups folder and, from the Action menu, select New Group.

   The New Group dialog box appears.

4. In the Group Name text box, type **ACCOUNTING**.

5. Click Add.

   The Select Users dialog box appears.

6. In the Enter The Object Names To Select box, type **DeborahP;CynthiaR** and click OK.

   The DeborahP and CynthiaR users are added to the new group's Members list.

7. Click Create, and then click Close.

   The ACCOUNTING group is added to the Groups folder.

8. Repeat steps 3 through 7 to create the BOOKKEEPING group and add the remaining three users as members.

9. Take a screen shot of the Computer Management console showing the contents of the Groups folder (by pressing ALT+PRT SCR), and paste it into a WordPad document named Computer*xx*Lab03-5.rtf (where *xx* is the number assigned to your computer by your instructor) to turn in at the end of the lab.

10. Close WordPad, the Computer Management console and the Administrative Tools window.

11. Log off Computer*xx*.

LAB REVIEW QUESTIONS

Estimated completion time: 15 minutes

1. In Exercise 3-1, you examined the local user accounts that already existed when you began this lab. How were these existing accounts created?

2. Based on your experiences logging on to Computerxx at the beginning of Exercise 3-1, what serious security problem existed on the system at that time? How did you remedy that problem?

3. In Exercise 3-2, why was it not necessary to assign a password to the Guest account?

4. In Exercise 3-5, how do you explain the difference between the group memberships for the JudyL and DeborahP accounts?

5. In Exercise 3-4, suppose the five users for whom you were required to create local user accounts on Computeryy already had accounts in the Contoso domain. Describe how you would be able to create all five users and create their appropriate group memberships (as described in Exercise 3-5) using only the User Accounts dialog box.

LAB CHALLENGE 3-1: CREATING DOMAIN USERS

Estimated completion time: 30 minutes

Domain user accounts are substantially different from local user accounts. While local user accounts are stored on the computer where they are created, domain user accounts are stored on a domain controller. Therefore, you must have access to a domain controller and use special administrative tools to create and manage domain accounts. To complete this challenge, you must log on to the Contoso domain, install the Windows Server 2003 Administrative Tools Pack, and use the tools to create user accounts in the domain.

1. On Computeryy, log on to the CONTOSO domain as Administrator, using the password **P@ssw0rd**.

2. Using Windows Explorer, browse to the Win2k3 share on the Server01 computer, execute Adminpak, a Windows Installer Package file, and follow the instructions in the Windows Server 2003 Administrative Tools Pack Setup Wizard.

3. Launch the Active Directory Users And Computers console (from the Administrative Tools program group).

4. Create a new organizational unit (OU) in the contoso.com domain called Computeryy, where *yy* is the number assigned to your computer.

5. Create a global security group called Computeryy in the Computeryy OU.

6. Create a new user in the Computeryy OU with your own name. Use **P@ssw0rd** for the password, and leave all the other settings at their default values.

7. Make the new user a member of the Computeryy group.

8. Take a screen shot (by pressing ALT+PRT SCR) of the Active Directory Users And Groups console showing the contents of the OU you created, and paste it into a WordPad document named ComputeryyLab03-6.rtf (where *yy* is the number assigned to your computer by your instructor) to turn in at the end of the lab.

9. Close The Active Directory Users And Computers console.

10. Log off Computeryy.

LAB 4
SUPPORTING THE WINDOWS DESKTOP

This lab contains the following exercises and activities:

- Exercise 4-1: Working with the Notification Area

- Exercise 4-2: Working with the Taskbar

- Exercise 4-3: Working with the Start Menu

- Exercise 4-4: Emulating the Windows 2000 Interface

- Exercise 4-5: Configuring Language Settings

- Lab Review Questions

- Lab Challenge 4-1: Disabling the Language Toggle

BEFORE YOU BEGIN

To complete this lab, you must have the following:

- The names (Computer*xx* and Computer*yy*) assigned to your computers by your instructor

SCENARIO

You are a new Microsoft Windows XP support technician for Contoso, Ltd., a company with workstations in a variety of environments. You are currently assigned to the desktop support help desk, and as a result, you are faced with a number of end-user problems related to the Windows XP desktop and interface.

After completing this lab, you will be able to:

- Manage icons in the notification area
- Configure the taskbar and Start menu

- Configure Windows XP to use the Microsoft Windows 2000 desktop
- Add alternate input languages

Estimated lesson time: 120 minutes

EXERCISE 4-1: WORKING WITH THE NOTIFICATION AREA

Estimated completion time: 15 minutes

A user calls the desktop support help desk, where you are working, and states that the icons in the notification area of his Windows XP workstation keep appearing and disappearing. After attempting to explain the default behavior of the notification area to the user, you decide that it would be easier to reconfigure his system so that the notification area icons do not hide themselves.

1. Log on to Computer*xx* as Administrator, using the password **P@ssw0rd**.

2. Right-click any open area on the taskbar, and select Task Manager.

3. Minimize the Task Manager window.

   Observe the CPU Usage icon in the notification area.

4. Right-click any empty spot on the taskbar or in the notification area, and select Properties.

   The Taskbar And Start Menu Properties dialog box appears.

5. In the Notification Area section, click Customize.

   The Customize Notifications dialog box appears.

6. In the Current Items area, click the Hide When Inactive value for the CPU Usage item.

   The Hide When Inactive value turns into a drop-down list.

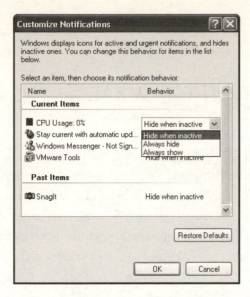

7. Select Always Hide, and click OK.

8. In the Taskbar And Start Menu Properties dialog box, make sure that the Show The Clock check box is selected. Then click OK.

> **QUESTION**   What happens?

9. Click the Arrow button in the notification area.

> **QUESTION**   What happens?

10. Move your cursor outside of the notification area, and wait a few seconds.

> **QUESTION**   What happens?

> **NOTE**   **Hiding Notification Area Icons**   Notification area icons can be hidden, but the programs they represent are still active, running in the background.

11. Open the Taskbar And Start Menu Properties dialog box, click Customize, and in the Customize Notifications dialog box, change the Behavior value for all the items to Always Show. Then click OK twice.

> **QUESTION**   What happens now?

12. Close Windows Task Manager.

13. Log off Computer*xx*.

EXERCISE 4-2: WORKING WITH THE TASKBAR

Estimated completion time: 15 minutes

Judy Lew, a new employee at Contoso, Ltd. calls the desktop help desk and asks you why her computer does not have the "little buttons next to the Start menu" with which she can launch her programs, and why the taskbar doesn't "go away" when she's not using it. She also states that she prefers to have the taskbar at the top of the screen, but she cannot move it. And finally, she is confused by the fact that when she has multiple Microsoft Internet Explorer windows open, only one instance appears on the taskbar. She wants you to come over and set her workstation up for her so that it is the same as her workstation at her last job.

1. On Computer*xx*, log on as JudyL, using the password **P@ssw0rd**.

   A Logon Message box appears to tell you that your password must be changed at first logon.

2. Click OK.

3. In the Change Password dialog box, type **P@ssw0rd** in the New Password and the Confirm New Password text boxes, and then click OK.

   A Change Password message box appears to tell you that the password has been changed.

4. Click OK.

5. Place your cursor anywhere in the taskbar, and then click and drag the taskbar to the top of the screen.

   QUESTION   *What happens?*

6. Right-click the taskbar and, on the context menu, click Lock The Taskbar to clear the check mark there.

7. Retry step 2.

   QUESTION   *What happens now?*

8. Right-click the taskbar and, on the context menu, select Properties.

The Taskbar And Start Menu Properties dialog box appears.

9. Select the Show Quick Launch check box, and click OK.

The Quick Launch area appears on the left in the taskbar.

> **QUESTION**   What icons appear in the Quick Launch area by default?

10. In the Quick Launch area, right-click the Internet Explorer icon and, from the context menu, select Delete.

A Confirm File Delete message box appears, asking you to confirm the deletion of the icon.

11. Click Yes.

The Internet Explorer icon is deleted from the Quick Launch area.

> **NOTE   Deleting Quick Launch Icons**   The Quick Launch area contains only shortcuts, not actual programs. Deleting an icon from the Quick Launch area does not affect the actual program launched by the icon, only the shortcut that points to the program.

12. Click Start, right-click the Microsoft Outlook Express icon on the Start menu, and drag it to the Quick Launch toolbar.

13. From the menu that appears, select Create Shortcuts Here.

14. An Outlook Express icon appears in the Quick Launch toolbar.

15. Using the same technique, add Notepad, Calculator, and Microsoft Paint to the Quick Launch toolbar.

> **NOTE   Copying Shortcuts**   If, when you drag an icon to the Quick Launch toolbar, the menu does not include a Create Shortcuts Here option, select Copy Here instead.

> **QUESTION**   How many icons appear in the Quick Launch area?

16. Click the dotted line at the right side of the Quick Launch area, and drag it an inch to the right.

> **QUESTION**   How many icons appear in the Quick Launch area now?

17. Click Start, and from the Start menu, click the Internet Explorer icon.

18. Repeat the previous step four times to open a total of five Internet Explorer windows.

> **QUESTION** How many program buttons appear on the taskbar (excluding the Quick Launch and notification areas)?

19. Open the Taskbar And Start Menu Properties dialog box.

20. Clear the Group Similar Taskbar Buttons check box, and click OK.

> **QUESTION** What happens?

21. Take a screen shot of the entire Windows screen (by pressing PRT SCR), and then paste it into a WordPad document named ComputerxxLab04-1.rtf (where *xx* is the number assigned to your computer by your instructor) to turn in at the end of the lab.

22. Open the Taskbar And Start Menu Properties dialog box.

23. Select the Auto-Hide The Taskbar check box, and click OK.

> **QUESTION** What happens?

24. Open the Taskbar And Start Menu Properties dialog box, select the Lock The Taskbar check box, and click OK.

25. Close all the Internet Explorer windows.

26. Log off the computer.

EXERCISE 4-3: WORKING WITH THE START MENU

Estimated completion time: 15 minutes

A new shipment of Windows XP workstations has arrived at Contoso, Ltd., with the operating system already installed by the manufacturer. Your task is to configure the Start menu on these computers so that the users have easy access to the programs they need, and so that they are insulated from components that management would prefer they avoid. In this exercise, you configure the Start menu to contain a set of specific programs rather than the most-recently used programs that appear there by default.

1. On Computeryy, log on to the local system as Administrator, using the password **P@ssw0rd**.

2. Open the Taskbar And Start Menu Properties dialog box, and click the Start menu tab.

3. With the default Start Menu option selected, click Customize.

    The Customize Start Menu dialog box appears.

4. In the Select An Icon Size For Programs group box, select the Small Icons option.

5. In the Programs group box, change the Number Of Programs On Start Menu box to 0. Then click Clear List.

6. Click the Advanced tab.

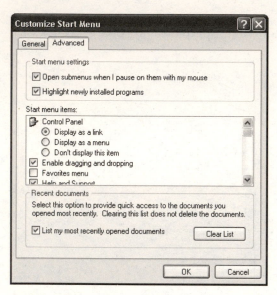

7. In the Start Menu Settings group box, clear the Highlight Newly Installed Programs check box.

8. In the Start Menu Items list box, modify the display options as follows:

❑ Control Panel: select the Display As A Menu option

❑ My Computer: select the Don't Display This Item option

❑ My Documents: select the Display As A Menu option

❑ My Music: select the Don't Display This Item option

❑ My Network Places: select this check box

❑ My Pictures: select the Don't Display This Item option

❑ Run Command: clear this check box

9. Click OK to close the Customize Start Menu dialog box.

10. Click OK to close the Taskbar And Start Menu Properties dialog box.

11. Click Start, point to All Programs, point to Accessories, right-click Calculator, and from the context menu, select Pin To Start Menu.

> **QUESTION**   What happens?

12. Use the same procedure to add the following programs to the Start menu:

   ❏ Notepad

   ❏ Paint

   ❏ Windows Explorer

   ❏ Wordpad

   ❏ Windows Media Player

13. Take a screen shot of the entire Windows screen (by pressing PRT SCR), showing the Start menu, and then paste it into a WordPad document named ComputeryyLab04-2.rtf (where yy is the number assigned to your computer by your instructor) to turn in at the end of the lab.

14. Close any open windows.

15. Log off the computer.

EXERCISE 4-4: EMULATING THE WINDOWS 2000 INTERFACE

Estimated completion time: 10 minutes

A user whose workstation was recently upgraded from Windows 2000 Professional Edition to Windows XP Professional Edition is complaining that she does not like the appearance of the Start menu or the taskbar. The user says that she was accustomed to the Windows 2000 layout and the changes in the Windows XP interface are slowing her down. She wants you to reconfigure her computer so that it uses the same interface as Windows 2000.

1. Log on to Computer**xx** using the DeborahP account you created in Exercise 3-3, using the password **P@ssw0rd**.

2. When prompted to do so, change the password to **P@ssw0rd**.

3. Open the Taskbar And Start Menu Properties dialog box, and click the Start Menu tab.

4. Select the Classic Start Menu option, and click Customize.

The Customize Classic Start Menu dialog box appears.

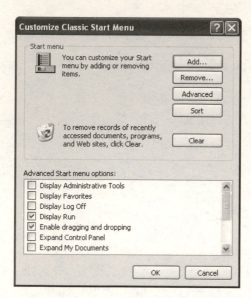

5. In the Advanced Start Menu Options box, configure the following settings:

❑ Select the Display Logoff check box

❑ Clear the Display Run check box

❑ Select the Expand Control Panel check box

❑ Select the Expand My Documents check box

❑ Clear the Use Personalized Menus check box

6. Click OK to close the Customize Classic Start Menu dialog box.

7. Click OK to close the Taskbar And Start Menu Properties dialog box.

> **QUESTION**   *How close have you come to fulfilling the user's request?*

8. Click Start, point to Settings, point to Control Panel, and select Display.

The Display Properties dialog box appears.

9. Click the Appearance tab.

10. In the Windows And Buttons drop-down list, select Windows Classic Style and click OK.

> **QUESTION** Now how close have you come to fulfilling the user's request?

11. Take a screen shot of the entire Windows screen (by pressing PRT SCR), showing the Start menu, and then paste it into a WordPad document named Computer*xx*Lab04-3.rtf (where *xx* is the number assigned to your computer by your instructor) to turn in at the end of the lab.

12. Log off the computer.

EXERCISE 4-5: CONFIGURING LANGUAGE SETTINGS

Estimated completion time: 20 minutes

Contoso, Ltd. has recently taken on a large contract for a client located in Ukraine. As a result, the company has hired a new employee, Cynthia Randall, who is fluent in Russian, to handle the communications and correspondence with the new client. You have been assigned the task of configuring a workstation for Ms. Randall that can accommodate her bilingual needs. In this exercise, you configure Windows XP to accept input in two languages.

1. On Computer*xx*, log on using the CynthiaR account you created in Exercise 3-3, with the password **P@ssw0rd**.

2. When prompted to do so, change the password to **P@ssw0rd**.

3. Open Control Panel, and click Date, Time, Language, And Regional Options.

The Date, Time, Language, And Regional Options page appears.

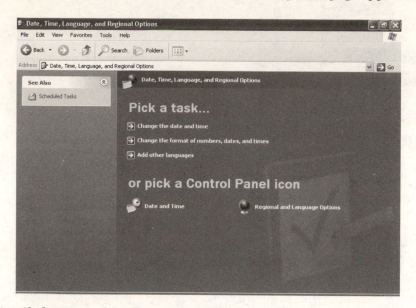

4. Click Regional And Language Options.

The Regional And Language Options dialog box appears.

5. Click the Languages tab.

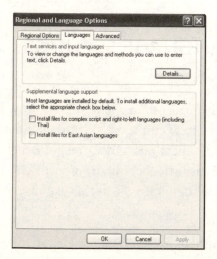

6. Click Details.

The Text Services And Input Languages dialog box appears.

7. Click Add.

The Add Input Language dialog box appears.

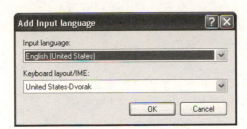

8. In the Input Language drop-down list, select Russian and click OK.

9. A Russian icon appears in the Installed Services list.

10. Click OK to close the Text Services And Input Languages dialog box.

11. Click OK to close the Regional And Language Options dialog box.

12. Close the Date, Time, Language, And Regional Options window.

13. Click Start, point to All Programs, point to Accessories, and then choose Notepad.

    The Notepad window appears.

14. In the Notepad window, type **All Work And No Play Makes Jack A Dull Boy**.

    QUESTION   *What happens?*

15. Press the left ALT+SHIFT key combination, and then type the same sentence again.

    QUESTION   *What happens now?*

16. Take a screen shot of the Notepad window (by pressing ALT+ PRT SCR), and then paste it into a WordPad document named Computer*xx*Lab04-4.rtf (where *xx* is the number assigned to your computer by your instructor) to turn in at the end of the lab.

17. Press the left ALT+SHIFT key combination again.

    The input language changes back to English.

18. Close Notepad.

19. Click No when asked if you want to save changes.

20. Log off the computer.

LAB REVIEW QUESTIONS

Estimated completion time: 15 minutes

1. A user tells you that he recently installed some new software that added an icon to the Quick Launch area of his taskbar. However, the Quick Launch bar is not big enough to display the additional icon, and

he has to press a button with two "right arrows" to access the additional icon. He wants to enlarge the Quick Launch bar, but he cannot seem to do so by dragging its right edge. In fact, he says he cannot even see the right edge. What should you tell the customer?

2. How can users switch input languages in Windows XP if you disable the ALT+SHIFT key combination?

3. In Exercise 4-1, you configured the notification area to hide specific icons when they are not in use. Hiding icons does not disable them, however; the programs they represent continue to run in the background. How do you disable an icon in the notification area so that the program does not run?

4. In Exercise 4-2, why is it that some icons, when you drag them to the Quick Launch area, have a Create Shortcuts Here option and others do not?

LAB CHALLENGE 4-1: DISABLING THE LANGUAGE TOGGLE

Estimated completion time: 30 minutes

Cynthia Randall, the employee at Contoso, Ltd. for whom you configured the alternate input language, is having problems because she is accidentally triggering the ALT+SHIFT key combination. She would like you to disable the ALT+SHIFT key combination because she uses the taskbar button to change languages. To complete this challenge, write out the procedure you would use to disable the ALT+SHIFT hot key and take a screen shot (by pressing ALT+PRT SCR) of the dialog box containing the control that disables the key combination. Then paste the screen shot into a WordPad document named ComputerxxLab04-5.rtf (where *xx* is the number assigned to your computer by your instructor) to turn in at the end of the lab.

1. Log on to Computerxx using the CynthiaR account.

2. Open Control Panel, and select Date, Time, Language, And Regional Options.

3. In the Date, Time, Language, And Regional Options window, select Regional And Language Options.

4. In the Regional And Language Options dialog box, on the Languages tab, click Details.

5. In the Text Services And Input Languages dialog box, click Key Settings.

    The Advanced Key Settings dialog box appears.

6. Click Change Key Sequence.

    The Change Key Sequence dialog box appears.

7. Clear the Switch Input Languages check box, and click OK.

8. Click OK to close the Advanced Key Settings dialog box.

9. Click OK to close the Text Services And Input Languages dialog box.

10. Click OK to close the Regional And Language Options dialog box.

11. Close the Date, Time, Language, And Regional Options window.

LAB 5
SUPPORTING FILE AND FOLDER ACCESS

This lab contains the following exercises and activities:

- Exercise 5-1: Configuring Folder Options

- Exercise 5-2: Configuring File Associations

- Exercise 5-3: Compressing Files and Folders

- Exercise 5-4: Using Simple File Sharing

- Exercise 5-5: Creating a Standard Share

- Exercise 5-6: Assigning NTFS Permissions

- Lab Review Questions

- Lab Challenge 5-1: Encrypting Folders

BEFORE YOU BEGIN

To complete this lab, you must have the following information:

- The names (Computerxx and Computeryy) assigned to your computers by your instructor.

SCENARIO

You are a Microsoft Windows XP support technician for Contoso, Ltd., a company with workstations in a variety of environments. You are currently assigned to the desktop support help desk, and as a result, you are faced with a number of problems concerning file sharing and access control.

After completing this lab, you will be able to:
- **Configure folder options**
- **Compress files**

- Create shares and assign share permissions
- Assign NTFS file system (NTFS) permissions

Estimated lesson time: 135 minutes

EXERCISE 5-1: CONFIGURING FOLDER OPTIONS

Estimated completion time: 15 minutes

You are a systems administrator for Contoso, Ltd. who has been given the task of configuring several new Windows XP computers for the network support staff. Because these users have more computing experience than most other company employees, you will be configuring the Windows interface to provide the users with greater access to the operating system than you would for other users. In this exercise, you modify the folder options on a computer to display file extensions and hidden files.

1. On Computeryy, log on using the local Administrator account, with the password **P@ssw0rd**.

2. Click Start, and then click Windows Explorer.

   A Windows Explorer window appears.

3. In the left pane, expand the My Computer node and click the Local Disk (C:) icon.

   QUESTION   What happens?

4. On the C: drive, click the Windows folder. Then, in the right pane, click the Show The Contents Of This Folder link.

   QUESTION   What happens?

5. From the View menu, select Details.

   Windows Explorer changes to a columnar display.

6. Locate a file in the C:\Windows folder called Blue Lace 16.

   QUESTION   What type of file is Blue Lace 16? How can you tell?

   QUESTION   Based only on the information in the Windows Explorer display, can you tell what the file extension of Blue Lace 16 is?

7. Open Control Panel, and select Folder Options.

The Folder Options dialog box appears.

8. On the General tab, in the Tasks group box, select the Use Windows Classic Folders option.

9. In the Browse Folders group box, verify that Open Each Folder In The Same Window is selected.

10. Click the View tab.

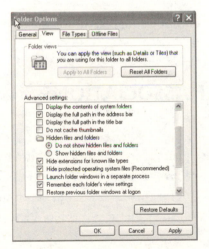

11. In the Advanced Settings list, make the following modifications:

    a. Select the Display The Contents Of System Folders check box.

    b. Select the Display The Full Path In The Title Bar check box.

    c. Select the Show Hidden Files And Folders option.

    d. Clear the Hide Extensions For Known File Types check box.

     e. Clear the Hide Protected Operating System Files (Recommended) check box, answering Yes when the Warning message box appears.

     f. Clear the Remember Each Folder's View Settings check box.

12. Click OK.

13. Return to the Windows Explorer window, and click the Local Disk (C:) icon.

> **QUESTION**   What happens now?

14. Click the Windows folder, and locate the Blue Lace 16 file you looked at earlier.

> **QUESTION**   What has changed about the Blue Lace 16 file?

15. Take a screen shot of the Windows Explorer window (by pressing ALT+PRT SCR) showing the contents of the C: drive, and paste it into a WordPad document named ComputeryyLab05-1.rtf (where yy is the number assigned to your computer by your instructor) to turn in at the end of the lab.

16. Leave Windows Explorer open and the computer logged on for the next exercise.

EXERCISE 5-2: CONFIGURING FILE ASSOCIATIONS

Estimated completion time: 15 minutes

Sally, an employee at Contoso, Ltd., has been given a large number of bitmap files by her supervisor, who has instructed her to rotate each file 90 degrees and then print it out. She plans to use Microsoft Paint for this task, but she has found that Windows XP opens bitmap files in the Windows Picture And Fax Viewer application by default. Sally calls the desktop support help desk where you are working and asks you to fix her computer so that she can double-click a bitmap file and have it open in Paint. In this exercise, you modify the file association for bitmap files on Sally's computer.

1. On Computeryy, in Windows Explorer, double-click the Blue Lace 16.bmp file from the previous exercise.

   QUESTION   What happens?

2. Close the Windows Picture And Fax Viewer window.

3. From the Tools menu, select Folder Options.

   The Folder Options dialog box appears. This is the same dialog box you accessed from Control Panel in Exercise 5-1.

4. Click the File Types tab.

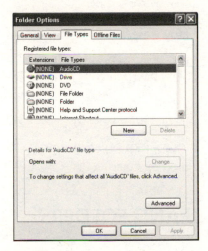

5. In the Registered File Types list, scroll down and select the BMP extension.

6. In the Details For BMP Extension group box, click Change.

The Open With dialog box appears.

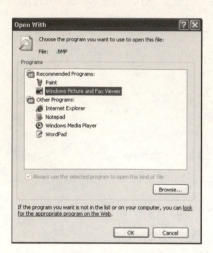

7. In the Programs group box, under Recommended Programs, click Paint, and then click OK.

8. Click Close to close the Folder Options dialog box.

9. Double-click the Blue Lace 16.bmp file again.

> **QUESTION**   What happens now?

10. Close the Paint window, but leave the Windows Explorer window open and the computer logged on for the next exercise.

EXERCISE 5-3: COMPRESSING FILES AND FOLDERS

Estimated completion time: 15 minutes

A user named Richard calls the desktop support help desk where you are working and tells you that he has to copy a number of large image files to his local drive, but an error has appeared on his computer, stating that he does not have enough disk space. Richard claims that he needs all the files on his hard disk and that there is nothing he can delete to make room for the new files. You decide to compress some of the files on Richard's drive to provide him with more space. In this exercise, you create a compressed folder and demonstrate the effects of copying and moving files to and from that folder.

1. On Computeryy, *in* Windows Explorer, click the Local Disk (C:) icon.

2. On the File menu, point to New and click Folder.

    A new folder appears on the C: drive.

3. Give the new folder the name **Documents**.

4. In the left pane, click the C:\Windows folder.

    The files in the Windows folder appear in the right pane.

5. Ensure that the Details view is selected for this folder, and then, in the right pane, click the Type column heading to sort the files in the folder by file type.

6. Scroll down in the right pane until you reach the bitmap images in the Windows folder.

7. Select all the BMP files in the C:\Windows folder, and copy them to the Documents folder you just created.

8. In the left pane, select the Documents folder and, from the File menu, select Properties.

The Documents Properties dialog box appears.

QUESTION   How many files are there in the Documents folder?

QUESTION   What is the Size value for the Documents folder?

QUESTION   What is the Size On Disk value of the Documents folder?

9. Click Advanced.

The Advanced Attributes dialog box appears.

10. In the Compress Or Encrypt Attributes group box, select the Compress Contents To Save Disk Space check box. Then click OK.

11. Click OK again to close the Documents Properties dialog box.

The Confirm Attribute Changes dialog box appears, prompting you to confirm whether you want to compress only the Documents folder or its subfolders and files as well.

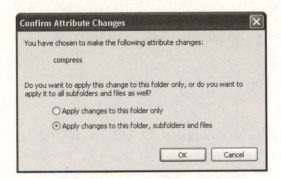

12. Click OK to accept the default value.

> **QUESTION**   What happens in Windows Explorer?

13. Open the Documents Properties dialog box again.

> **QUESTION**   What indication do you have in the Documents Properties dialog box that the folder and its contents have been compressed?

14. Take a screen shot of the Documents Properties dialog box (by pressing ALT+PRT SCR) showing the reduced Size On Disk value, and paste it into a WordPad document named ComputeryyLab05-2.rtf (where yy is the number assigned to your computer by your instructor) to turn in at the end of the lab.

15. Click OK to close the Documents Properties dialog box.

16. In the Documents folder, select one of the compressed files and move it to the root of the C: drive.

> **QUESTION**   Is the file still compressed? How can you tell?

17. Select another file from the Documents folder, and copy it to the root of the C: drive.

> **QUESTION** *Is the copied file still compressed?*

18. On the root of the C: drive, select the Ntdetect.com file and copy it to the Documents folder.

> **NOTE** *Copying vs. Moving* *Be sure to copy the Ntdetect.com file. Do not move it.*

> **QUESTION** *Is the copy of the Ntdetect.com file compressed or not?*

19. Close Windows Explorer, but leave the computer logged on for the next exercise.

EXERCISE 5-4: USING SIMPLE FILE SHARING

Estimated completion time: 15 minutes

Mary Ann, a user working from home, calls you at the desktop support help desk for assistance. She has two Windows XP Professional Edition computers in her home that are networked together using wireless local area network (LAN) technology so that both systems can access one printer. Mary Ann says that her work files are located on the computer in her home office, but she wants to access them using the laptop in the bedroom. Because security is not a concern, you decide to walk Mary Ann through the process of sharing her files, using the Simple File Sharing feature that Windows XP Professional Edition defaults to when it is not connected to a domain. In this exercise, you share a folder on one computer and access it from the other.

1. On Computer*xx*, log on as Administrator, using the password **P@ssw0rd**.

2. Click Start, and then click My Documents.

The My Documents window appears.

3. In the File And Folder Tasks box, click Make A New Folder and name the folder **Documents**.

4. Select the Documents folder you just created, and click Share This Folder.

The Documents Properties dialog box appears, with the Sharing tab selected.

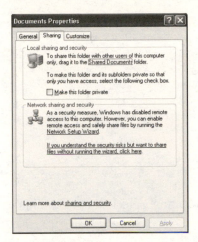

5. In the Network Sharing And Security group box, click the If You Understand The Security Risks But Want To Share Files Without Running The Wizard, Click Here link.

The Enable File Sharing dialog box appears.

6. Select the Just Enable File Sharing option, and click OK.

The controls on the Sharing tab of the Documents Properties dialog box change. On a computer running Windows XP RTM or Windows XP SP1, the dialog box appears as follows:

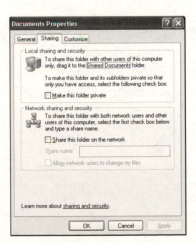

On a computer running Windows XP SP2, the dialog box appears as follows:

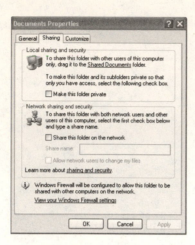

7. In the Network Sharing And Security group box, select the Share This Folder On The Network check box.

8. Leave the default Share Name value (Documents) in place, and make sure the Allow Network Users To Change My Files check box is selected. Then click OK.

9. On Computeryy, open Windows Explorer and, in the left pane, expand My Network Places down to Domainxxyy (where xx and yy are the numbers assigned to the computers in your student lab group), and select the Computerxx icon.

QUESTION *What do you see in the right pane?*

10. Take a screen shot of the Windows Explorer window (by pressing ALT+PRT SCR) on Computeryy showing the shared Documents folder on Computerxx, and paste it into a WordPad document named ComputeryyLab05-3.rtf (where yy is the number assigned to your computer by your instructor) to turn in at the end of the lab.

11. Log of Computeryy and leave Computerxx logged on for later exercises.

EXERCISE 5-5: CREATING A STANDARD SHARE

Estimated completion time: 15 minutes

Fred, a user with a Windows XP workstation in the Contoso.com domain, has files on his local drive that he must share with other users on the network. However, these files must not be fully accessible to everyone. As the desktop support technician responding to Fred's request, you decide to create a standard share on his computer and use share permissions to control access to the files. In this exercise, you create a standard share and assign appropriate permissions.

1. On Computeryy, log on to the Contoso domain as Administrator, using the password **P@ssw0rd**.

2. On Computeryy, in Windows Explorer, right-click the Documents folder you created in Exercise 5-3 and, on the context menu, select Sharing And Security.

   The Documents Properties dialog box appears, with the Sharing tab selected.

   On a computer running Windows XP RTM or Windows XP SP1, the dialog box appears as follows:

On a computer running Windows XP SP2, the dialog box appears as follows:

3. Select the Share This Folder option.

The default value Documents appears in the Share Name text box.

4. Click Permissions.

The Permissions For Documents dialog box appears.

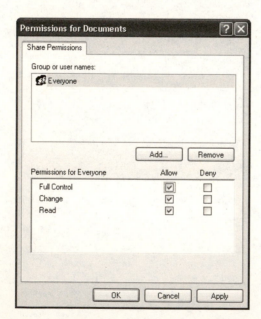

5. For the Everyone special identity, make sure that only the Read check box is selected in the Allow column.

6. Click Add.

The Select Users, Computers, Or Groups dialog box appears.

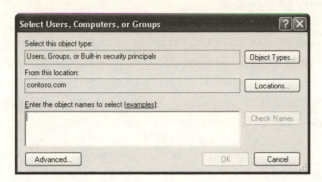

7. In the Enter The Object Names To Select box, type **Domain Admins** and click OK.

The Domain Admins group appears in the Group Or User Names list in the Permissions For Documents dialog box.

8. With the Domain Admins group highlighted, select the Full Control check box in the Allow column.

Selecting the Full Control check box causes the Change check box to be selected as well.

9. Using the same technique, add the Domain Users group to the Group Or User Names list and assign it the Allow Read permission only.

10. Take a screen shot of the Permissions For Documents dialog box (by pressing ALT+PRT SCR), and paste it into a WordPad document named ComputeryyLab05-4.rtf (where *yy* is the number assigned to your computer by your instructor) to turn in at the end of the lab.

11. Click OK to close the Permissions For Documents dialog box.

12. Click OK to close the Documents Properties dialog box.

13. On Computerxx, in Windows Explorer, browse to Computeryy in My Network Places and click the Documents share.

14. Select one of the files in the Documents share, and try to delete it.

QUESTION   *Were you successful? Why?*

15. Leave Windows Explorer open and the computers logged on for later exercises.

EXERCISE 5-6: ASSIGNING NTFS PERMISSIONS

Estimated completion time: 15 minutes

You are a network administrator who has been assigned the task of setting up a kiosk computer on which various users can read Human Resources documents. You decide to use the Guest account on the computer for this purpose and provide that account with limited access to the documents by using NTFS permissions. In this exercise, you create NTFS permission assignments for a folder and view the effective permissions for the Guest user.

1. On Computeryy, in Windows Explorer, select the Documents folder you created in Exercise 5-3 and open its Properties dialog box.

2. Click the Security tab.

3. Click Add.

    The Select Users, Computers, Or Groups dialog box appears.

4. In the Enter The Object Names To Select box, type **Guest** and click OK.

    The Guest account is added to the Group Or User Names list in the Documents Properties dialog box.

5. Select the Guest account.

6. In the Permissions For Guest box, clear the Allow check boxes for all except the Read permission.

7. Click Apply.

The Guest account now has Read permissions for the Documents folder.

8. Click Advanced.

The Advanced Security Settings For Documents dialog box appears.

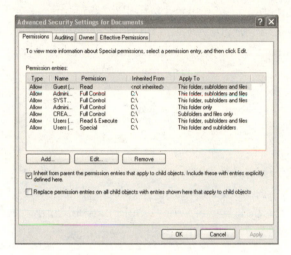

9. Click the Effective Permissions tab.

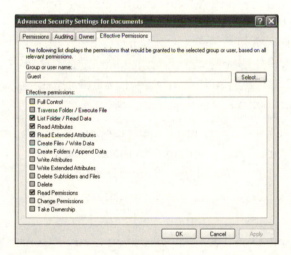

10. Click Select.

   The Select Users, Computers, Or Groups dialog box appears.

11. Type **Guest** and click OK.

   The effective permissions for the guest user appear in the Effective Permissions dialog box.

12. Take a screen shot of the Advanced Security Settings For Documents dialog box (by pressing ALT+PRT SCR) showing the effective permissions for the Guest account, and paste it into a WordPad document named ComputeryyLab05-5.rtf (where yy is the number assigned to your computer by your instructor) to turn in at the end of the lab.

13. Log off of Computeryy.

LAB REVIEW QUESTIONS

Estimated completion time: 15 minutes

1. In Exercise 5-3, you compressed a folder on the Windows XP C: drive to provide the user with more disk space. What would have been the result if the user's drive was formatted using the FAT32 file system instead of NTFS?

2. On Computeryy, log on using the local Administrator account, open the Folder Options dialog box, click the View tab, and clear the Use Simple File Sharing (Recommended) check box. Select a folder on the C: drive, open its Properties dialog box, and click the Sharing tab. How has the sharing interface changed from the one you used in Exercise 5-5? How can you explain this behavior?

3. In Exercise 5-6, you used the Security tab in a folder's Properties dialog box on Computeryy to assign NTFS permissions to that folder. What happens when you try to do the same thing on Computerxx? Why?

4. In Exercise 5-5, why is the interface shown on the Sharing tab of the Documents Properties dialog box on Computeryy different from the Sharing tab of the Documents Properties dialog box you used on Computerxx in Exercise 5-4?

LAB CHALLENGE 5-1: ENCRYPTING FOLDERS

Estimated completion time: 30 minutes

Richard, the user from Exercise 5-3, calls the help desk and tells you that he is storing some extremely confidential company files on his computer. He is wondering whether there aren't some extraordinary security measures he can take to ensure that no one but the local Administrator account can access these files. Richard also informs you that he has resolved his earlier disk space problem by archiving some files to CD-ROMs. To complete this challenge, you must configure the Documents folder on Richard's computer (Computeryy) to use the Encrypting File System and write out the procedure you used to perform this configuration. Then, test your work by attempting to access one of the files in the Documents folder from Computerxx. Take a screen shot of the message box denying you access to the file (by pressing ALT+PRT SCR), and paste it into a WordPad document named ComputerxxLab05-6.rtf (where xx is the number assigned to your computer by your instructor), to turn in at the end of the lab.

Close all open windows and log off both computers.

LAB 6

INSTALLING AND MANAGING HARDWARE

This lab contains the following exercises and activities:

- Exercise 6-1: Using the Add New Hardware Wizard

- Exercise 6-2: Using the System Information Tool

- Exercise 6-3: Using Device Manager

- Exercise 6-4: Configuring Local Driver Signature Settings

- Exercise 6-5: Scanning for Unsigned Drivers

- Lab Review Questions

- Lab Challenge 6-1: Configuring Driver Signature Settings with Group Policies

BEFORE YOU BEGIN

To complete this lab, you must have the following information:

- The names (Computer*xx* and Computer*yy*) assigned to your computers by your instructor

SCENARIO

You are a Microsoft Windows XP support technician for Contoso, Ltd., a company with workstations in a variety of environments. You are currently working on deploying a number of computers for new employees, and as a result, you are faced with a number of hardware administration tasks.

After completing this lab, you will be able to:

- Add new hardware to a Windows XP computer
- View and manage device settings using the System Information tool and Device Manager
- Locate and prohibit unsigned driver installations

Estimated lesson time: 110 minutes

EXERCISE 6-1: USING THE ADD NEW HARDWARE WIZARD

Estimated completion time: 15 minutes

You are a Windows XP system support specialist who has been assigned the task of preparing a number of new workstations for deployment on the company network. You must prepare the workstations to use a printer, even though the printer is not yet connected. In this exercise, you manually install a printer driver by using the Add New Hardware Wizard.

1. Log on to Computer*xx* as Administrator (where *xx* is the number assigned to your computer), using the password **P@ssw0rd**.

2. Click Start, and open Control Panel.

3. Click Printers And Other Hardware.

   The Printers And Other Hardware window appears.

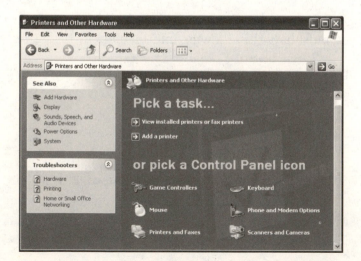

4. In the See Also box, click Add Hardware.

The Welcome To The Add Hardware Wizard page appears.

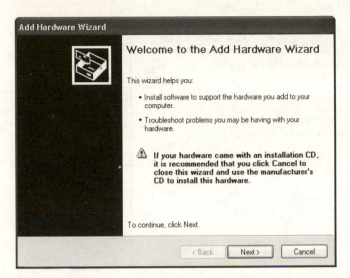

5. Click Next.

The Add Hardware Wizard searches for new Plug and Play devices, and then displays the Is The Hardware Connected? page.

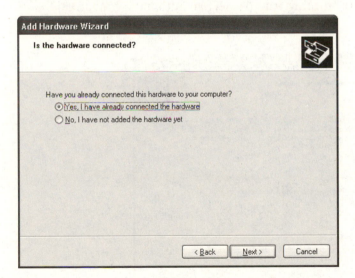

6. Select Yes, I Have Already Connected The Hardware, and then click Next.

A list of the hardware installed on the computer appears.

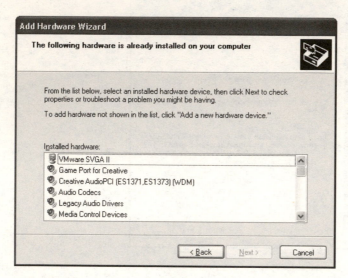

7. Scroll to the bottom of the list, select Add A New Hardware Device, and click Next.

A page appears prompting you to select an automatic or manual installation.

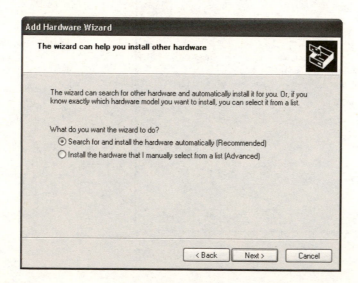

8. Select Install The Hardware That I Manually Select From A List (Advanced), and click Next.

A list of hardware device types appears.

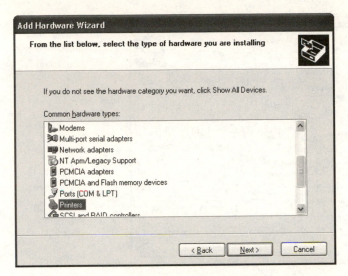

9. Scroll down in the list, select Printers, and click Next.

The Select A Printer Port page appears.

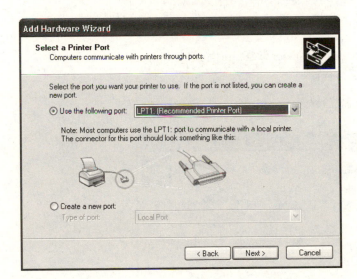

10. In the Use The Following Port drop-down list, select LPT2: (Printer Port), and then click Next.

The Install Printer Software page appears.

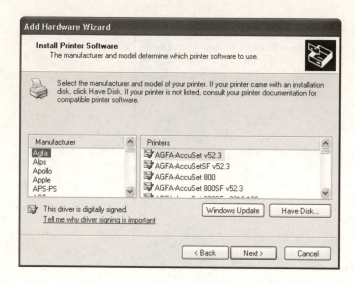

> **NOTE   Using Windows XP SP2**   If you are running Windows XP SP2, the Install Printer Software page does not include the Windows Update button.

11. In the Manufacturer list, select HP. In the Printers list, select HP Laser-Jet 5. Then, click Next.

The Name Your Printer page appears.

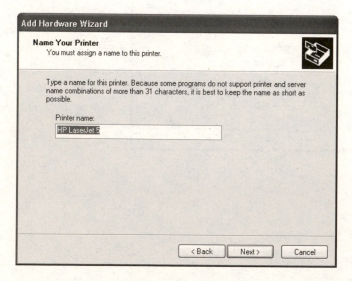

12. Click Next to accept the default printer name.

The Printer Sharing page appears.

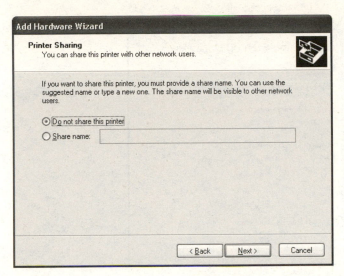

13. Click Next to accept the default Do Not Share This Printer setting.

The Print Test Page page appears.

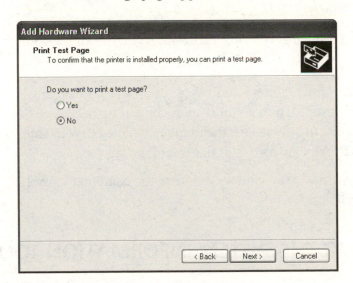

14. Select No and then click Next.

The Completing The Add Hardware Wizard page appears.

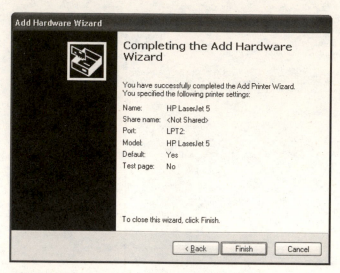

15. Click Finish.

16. On the Printers And Other Hardware window, click View Installed Printers Or Fax Printers.

The HP LaserJet 5 printer you just installed appears in the Printers And Faxes window.

17. Take a screen shot of the Printers And Faxes window (by pressing ALT+PRT SCR), and paste it into a WordPad document named Computer*xx*Lab06-1.rtf (where *xx* is the number assigned to your computer by your instructor) to turn in at the end of the lab.

18. Close the Printers And Faxes window and leave the computer logged on for the next exercise.

EXERCISE 6-2: USING THE SYSTEM INFORMATION TOOL

Estimated completion time: 15 minutes

A new graphics artist has been hired by Contoso, Ltd., and you are the system administrator who has been assigned the task of preparing her workstation. You plan to install a higher-quality display adapter into the computer, but first you want to save a report on the system's hardware configuration in case there are problems later. In this exercise, you run the System Information tool and use it to save a report on the computer's hardware configuration.

1. On Computerxx, click Start, and then click Run.

    The Run dialog box appears.

2. In the Open text box, type **msinfo32** and press ENTER.

    The System Information window appears.

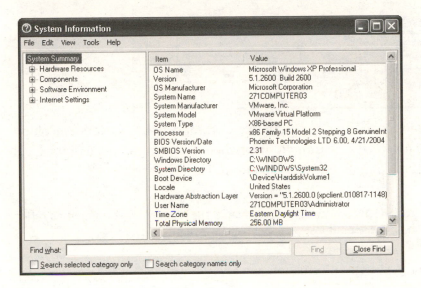

QUESTION   How much Total Physical Memory is there on the computer?

3. In the Find What text box, type **display** and click Find.

    QUESTION   What happens?

    QUESTION   What is the name of the display adapter installed in the computer?

4. From the File menu, select Save.

    The Save As dialog box appears.

5. In the File Name text box, type **Computerxx** and click Save.

    The program saves the system information to an NFO file.

6. From the File menu, select Export.

    The Export As dialog box appears.

7. In the File Name text box, type **Computerxx** and click Save.

The program saves the system information to a text file.

8. From the View menu, select Remote Computer.

The Remote Computer dialog box appears.

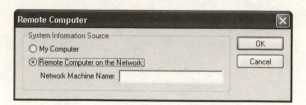

9. Select Remote Computer on the Network, and in the Network Machine Name text box, type **Computeryy**, where *yy* is the number assigned to the other computer in your lab group. Then click OK.

> **QUESTION**   How can you tell that the display has changed to reflect the other computer's system information?

10. Close the System Information window.

11. Leave the computer logged on for later exercises.

EXERCISE 6-3: USING DEVICE MANAGER

Estimated completion time: 15 minutes

You are a new system support technician at Contoso, Ltd., and you are attempting to troubleshoot a computer that is experiencing communication problems on the network. You think that the problem might be a hardware conflict between the network interface card you just installed, which was salvaged from an old machine, and the computer's printer port. To test your theory, you decide to disable the printer port temporarily. In this exercise, you use the Device Manager application to view the resources that the printer port is utilizing and then you disable the printer port.

1. On Computerxx, open Control Panel and select Performance And Maintenance.

The Performance And Maintenance window appears.

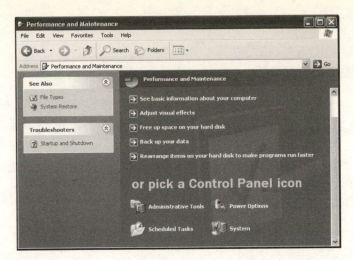

2. Click System.

   The System Properties dialog box appears.

3. Click the Hardware tab.

   If you are running Windows XP RTM or Windows XP SP1, the Hardware tab appears as follows:

If you are running Windows XP SP2, the Hardware tab appears as follows:

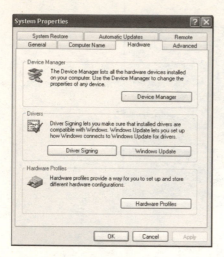

4. Click Device Manager.

The Device Manager window appears.

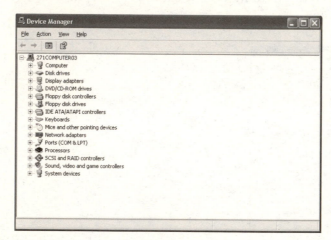

5. Expand the Ports (COM & LPT) heading.

6. Right-click the Printer Port (LPT1) item, and select Properties from the context menu.

The Printer Port (LPT1) Properties dialog box appears.

7. Click the Resources tab.

QUESTION   What resources is the port currently using?

8. Click the General tab.

9. In the Device Usage drop-down list, select Do Not Use This Device
    (Disable) and click OK.

QUESTION   What happens?

10. Open the Printer Port (LPT1) Properties dialog box again, and re-enable the port. Then click OK.

11. From the View menu, select Show Hidden Devices.

QUESTION   What happens to the Device Manager components list?

12. From the View menu, select Resources By Type.

The Device Manager display changes to a list of resource types.

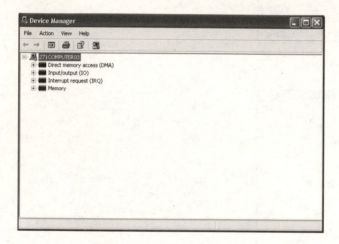

QUESTION   What input/output (I/O) resources is the computer's network interface adapter currently using?

13. Take a screen shot of the Device Manager window (by pressing ALT+PRT SCR) showing the I/O resources used by the network interface adapter, and paste it into a WordPad document named ComputerxxLab06-2.rtf (where *xx* is the number assigned to your computer by your instructor) to turn in at the end of the lab.

14. Close Device Manager and all other open windows, and leave the computer logged on for later exercises.

EXERCISE 6-4: CONFIGURING LOCAL DRIVER SIGNATURE SETTINGS

Estimated completion time: 10 minutes

After a recent incident in which an unsigned driver caused compatibility problems on dozens of computers, the IT director at Contoso, Ltd. has decided that all the drivers on the company's computers must be signed by Microsoft. Your job is to configure each computer to block the installation of unsigned drivers. In this exercise, you do this by using the System Properties dialog box.

1. On Computerxx, open the System Properties dialog box, as you did in Exercise 6-3.

2. Click the Hardware tab, and then click Driver Signing.

    The Driver Signing Options dialog box appears.

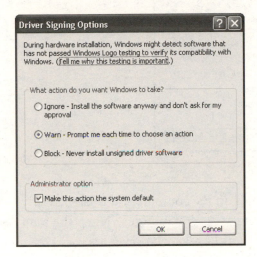

QUESTION   What is the computer's current setting?

3. Select the Block – Never Install Unsigned Driver Software option.

4. Make sure the Make This Action The System Default check box is selected, and click OK.

5. Click OK to close the System Properties dialog box.

6. Close the Performance And Maintenance window.

7. Leave the computer logged on for later exercises.

EXERCISE 6-5: SCANNING FOR UNSIGNED DRIVERS

Estimated completion time: 10 minutes

After a recent incident in which an unsigned driver caused compatibility problems on dozens of computers, the IT director at Contoso, Ltd. has decided that all the drivers on the company's computers must be signed by Microsoft. As a result, you have been given the task of identifying the unsigned drivers that must be replaced on all systems. In this exercise, you use the File Signature Verification tool to scan your computer for unsigned drivers.

1. On Computerxx, click Start and open the Run dialog box.

2. In the Open text box, type **sigverif** and click OK.

The File Signature Verification dialog box appears.

3. Click Start.

The program scans the system files on the computer for unsigned drivers, a process that can take as long as several minutes. When the scan is finished, the Signature Verification Results window appears.

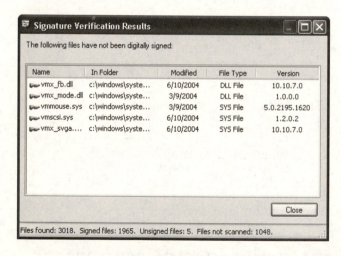

NOTE   Using Digitally Signed Drivers   If the program determines that all the driver files installed on your computer have been verified as digitally signed, then a SigVerif dialog box appears instead of the Signature Verification Results window.

QUESTION   How many unsigned drivers are there on your computer?

4. Click Close to close the Signature Verification Results window.

5. Click Close to close the File Signature Verification tool.

6. Log off the computer.

LAB REVIEW QUESTIONS

Estimated completion time: 15 minutes

1. In Exercise 6-1, why was it necessary to select the Yes, I Have Already Connected The Hardware option, even though you did not actually connect any new hardware?

2. In Exercise 6-1, how would the printer installation procedure differ if the printer was connected directly to the network rather than the computer?

3. In Exercise 6-2, what is the benefit of exporting the system information, as opposed to saving it?

4. In Exercise 6-5, why was it necessary to scan the computer for unsigned drivers when you already configured the system to block unsigned driver installations in Exercise 6-4?

LAB CHALLENGE 6-1: CONFIGURING DRIVER SIGNATURE SETTINGS WITH GROUP POLICIES

Estimated completion time: 30 minutes

After configuring the driver signature settings manually on several computers, you decide that this method is far too time consuming. Therefore, you decide to create a Group Policy Object (GPO) that will set a value for the Devices: Unsigned Driver Installation Behavior security option. To complete this challenge, you must log on to Computeryy and create a new GPO called Driver Signatures with the appropriate security option, without installing any additional software on Computeryy. Write out the procedure you used to create the GPO and take a screen shot of the GPO (by pressing ALT+PRT SCR) with the Devices: Unsigned Driver Installation Behavior security option highlighted. Then paste the screen shot into a WordPad document named ComputeryyLab06-3.rtf (where yy is the number assigned to your computer by your instructor) to turn in at the end of the lab.

LAB 7

SUPPORTING DISPLAY DEVICES, I/O DEVICES, AND ACPI

This lab contains the following exercises and activities:

■ Exercise 7-1: Configuring Display Properties

■ Exercise 7-2: Configuring Mouse Properties

■ Exercise 7-3: Configuring Modem Properties

■ Lab Review Questions

■ Lab Challenge 7-1: Adjusting Icon Text Size

BEFORE YOU BEGIN

To complete this lab, you must have the following information:

■ The names (Computer*xx* and Computer*yy*) assigned to your computers by your instructor

SCENARIO

You are a Microsoft Windows XP support technician for Contoso, Ltd., a company with workstations in a variety of environments. You are currently working the desktop support help desk, and you have received a number of calls this morning concerning various device configuration issues.

After completing this lab, you will be able to:

- Configure Windows XP display properties
- Configure Windows XP mouse properties
- Install and configure a modem in Windows XP

Estimated lesson time: 70 minutes

EXERCISE 7-1: CONFIGURING DISPLAY PROPERTIES

Estimated completion time: 20 minutes

Margaret, a new employee at Contoso, Ltd., calls the help desk saying that she needs assistance configuring her monitor. "The icons and everything are too big," she says. At her last job, she was able to display a whole page in Microsoft Word and still read the text comfortably, and she would like you to "fix her monitor" so that she can do that again. In addition, Margaret says that she will be working on confidential documents for her boss, but she finds it a chore to log off every time she steps away from the computer. She wants to know whether there is an easier way to secure her workstation. In this exercise, you modify the screen resolution in Windows XP and change the screen saver settings to satisfy Margaret's needs.

1. On Computer*xx*, log on as Administrator, using the password **P@ssw0rd**.

2. Open Control Panel, and click Appearance And Themes.

    The Appearance And Themes page appears.

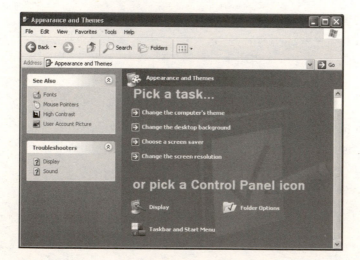

3. Click Display.

The Display Properties dialog box appears.

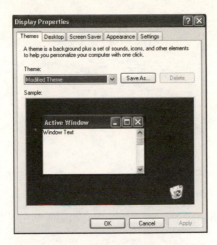

Click the Settings tab.

4. In the Screen Resolution group box, move the slider to the right to increase the resolution of the display. Then click Apply

A Monitor Settings message box appears, asking whether you want to keep the settings you selected. After 15 seconds, the display reverts back to its original screen resolution.

5. Click Advanced.

The Properties dialog box for your monitor and video display adapter appears.

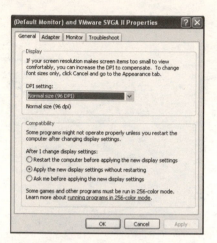

6. Click the Adapter tab.

QUESTION *What video adapter type is your computer using?*

7. Click List All Modes.

The List All Modes dialog box appears.

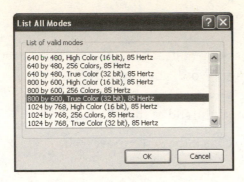

> **QUESTION**   What is the highest screen resolution supported by your monitor and video adapter?

8. Select the entry with a screen resolution of 640 × 480 and 16 colors. Then click OK.

9. In the Properties dialog box, click Apply.

10. When the Monitor Settings message box appears again, click Yes to accept the settings.

> **QUESTION**   What do you think Margaret's reaction will be to these modifications?

11. Open the List All Modes dialog box again.

12. Select the entry in the list with a resolution of 1024 × 768 and the highest available color depth. Then click OK.

> **NOTE   Understanding Color Depth Settings**   Color depth settings typically range from 16 colors (4-bit) at the low end to True Color (32-bit) at the high end.

13. In the monitor and adapter Properties dialog box, click OK.

14. When the Monitor Settings message box appears again, click Yes to accept the settings.

QUESTION   *How will Margaret react to these settings?*

15. Take a screen shot of the entire desktop at its new resolution (by pressing PRT SCR), and paste it into a WordPad document named Computer*xx*Lab07-1.rtf (where *xx* is the number assigned to your computer by your instructor) to turn in at the end of the lab.

16. In the Display Properties dialog box, click the Screen Saver tab.

17. Make sure that the Windows XP screen saver is selected in the drop-down list, and then change the Wait box value to 2.

18. Select the On Resume, Password Protect check box, and click OK.

19. Wait two minutes for the screen saver to appear. Do not touch the keyboard or the mouse.

20. Once the screen saver appears, press any key on the keyboard.

QUESTION   *What happens?*

21. In the Password text box, type **P@ssw0rd** and click OK.

The dialog box disappears, and the computer is unlocked.

22. Open the Display Properties dialog box again and click the Screen Saver tab.

23. Clear the On Resume, Password Protect check box, change the Wait box value to 10, and then click OK.

24. Close the Appearances And Themes window.

25. Leave the computer logged on for the next exercise.

EXERCISE 7-2: CONFIGURING MOUSE PROPERTIES

Estimated completion time: 15 minutes

Herb is an outside salesman at Contoso, Ltd. who works with a laptop computer that he likes very much although it is several years old. Over the years, the screen on Herb's laptop has become dimmer, and he is now having difficulty seeing the mouse cursor. Also, the mouse buttons on the computer sometimes stick, making it difficult for Herb to double-click icons. He calls the help desk asking whether you can help him to keep his beloved computer working for a while longer. In this exercise, you configure the mouse properties on a Windows XP computer to make the cursor more visible to the user.

1. On Computer*xx*, open Control Panel and click Printers And Other Hardware.

   The Printers And Other Hardware page appears.

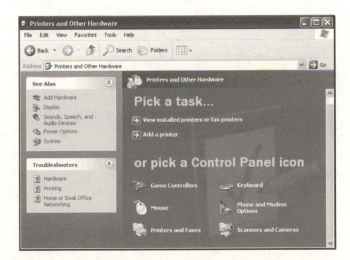

2. Click Mouse.

The Mouse Properties dialog box appears.

3. On the Buttons tab, in the Double-Click Speed group box, move the slider all the way to the right. Then test the result by double-clicking the folder icon.

> **QUESTION**   Will this adjustment help to solve Herb's double-clicking problem? Why or why not?

4. Now move the slider all the way to the left.

> **QUESTION**   Will this adjustment help to solve Herb's double-clicking problem? Why or why not?

5. Move the slider to the best position for Herb, and click Apply.

6. Click the Pointer Options tab.

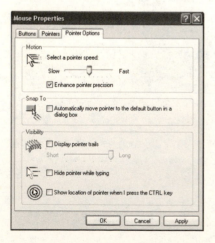

7. In the Motion group box, move the Select A Pointer Speed slider to its fastest and slowest settings, testing the behavior of the mouse at each extreme.

   > **QUESTION**   Will this adjustment make the mouse more usable for Herb? Why or why not?

   > **QUESTION**   Which of the controls in the Visibility group box would best help Herb to see the mouse cursor on his dim laptop screen? Why is the control you selected preferable to the others?

8. Click the Pointers tab.

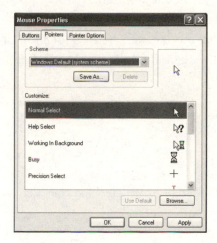

9. Open the drop-down list in the Scheme box.

   > **QUESTION**   Which scheme do you think would best help Herb to see the cursor on his laptop?

10. Select the scheme for Herb, and click Apply.

11. Take a screen shot of the Mouse Properties dialog box (by pressing ALT+PRT SCR), and paste it into a WordPad document named ComputerxxLab07-2.rtf (where xx is the number assigned to your computer by your instructor) to turn in at the end of the lab.

12. Click OK to close the Mouse Properties dialog box.

13. Close the Printers And Other Hardware window and leave the computer logged on for the next exercise.

EXERCISE 7-3: CONFIGURING MODEM PROPERTIES

Estimated completion time: 20 minutes

Mary Ann, a director at Contoso, Ltd., is leaving on a business trip next week, and you have been given the task of setting up a notebook computer for her to take on her journey. You are planning to install a modem in the laptop so that Mary Ann can dial into her Internet service provider (ISP) and access the company servers by using a virtual private network connection. However, the modem has not arrived from the supplier. Mary Ann's trip will take her to Seattle, New York, and Washington, D.C., and you want her to be able to place local calls to her ISP from each of those locations. In addition, Mary Ann has told you that because she often connects from libraries and other quiet work areas, she would like the connection process to be silent. In this exercise, you install the modem driver on the computer, even though you do not have the actual modem yet, create a location profile for each of the three cities Mary Ann will visit, and configure the modem to operate silently.

1. On Computerxx, open Control Panel and launch the Add Hardware Wizard.

    > **MORE INFO** **Adding New Hardware** See Lab 6, "Installing and Managing Hardware," to review the procedure for launching the Add Hardware Wizard.

2. When the Welcome To The Add Hardware Wizard page appears, click Next.

    The Add Hardware Wizard searches for new Plug and Play devices, and then displays the Is The Hardware Connected? page.

3. Select Yes, I Have Already Connected The Hardware, and then click Next.

    A list of the hardware installed on the computer appears.

    > **QUESTION** Why is it necessary to answer Yes to this question, even though the modem is not actually installed in the computer yet?

4. Scroll to the bottom of the list, select Add A New Hardware Device, and click Next.

    A page appears prompting you to select an automatic or manual installation.

5. Select Install The Hardware That I Manually Select From A List (Advanced), and click Next.

A list of hardware device types appears.

6. Scroll down in the list, select Modems, and click Next.

The Install New Modem: Do You Want Windows To Detect Your Modem? page appears.

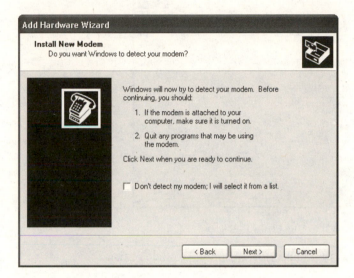

7. Select the Don't Detect My Modem; I Will Select It From A List check box, and click Next.

The Install New Modem page appears.

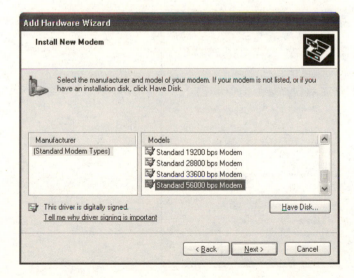

8. Scroll down in the Models list, select Standard 56000 bps Modem, and click Next.

The Install New Modem: Select The Port(s) You Want To Install The Modem On page appears.

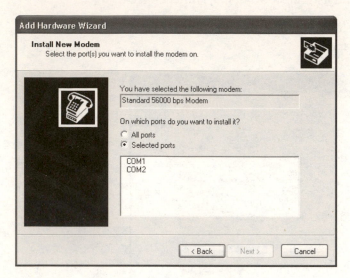

9. Select the COM2 port, and click Next.

10. When the modem installation is completed, click Finish.

11. On the Printers And Other Hardware Page, click Phone And Modem Options.

The Location Information dialog box appears.

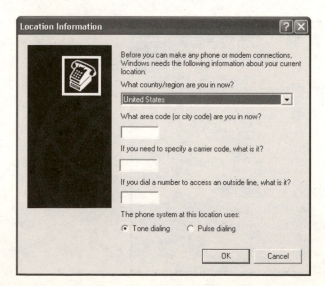

12. In the What Area Code (Or City Code) Are You In Now? text box, type **206** and click OK.

    After a few seconds, the Phone And Modem Options dialog box appears.

13. Click Edit.

    The Edit Location dialog box appears.

14. Change the value in the Location Name text box to **Seattle**, and click OK.

15. Click New.

The New Location dialog box appears.

16. In the Location Name text box, type **Washington, DC**.

17. In the Area Code text box, type **202**.

18. In the Dialing Rules box, type **9** in the To Access An Outside Line For Local Calls, Dial: text box. Then click OK.

19. Create another new location, using the following information:

- ❑ Location Name: **New York**

- ❑ Area Code: **212**

20. Take a screen shot of the Phone And Modem Options dialog box (by pressing ALT+PRT SCR) showing the three locations you have created, and paste it into a WordPad document named Computer*xx*Lab07-3.rtf (where *xx* is the number assigned to your computer by your instructor) to turn in at the end of the lab.

21. In the Phone And Modem Options dialog box, click the Modems tab.

22. Click Properties.

The Standard 56000 bps Modem Properties dialog box appears.

23. Click the Modem tab.

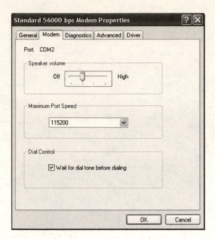

24. In the Speaker Volume box, move the slider all the way to the left.

25. Click the Diagnostics tab.

> **QUESTION**   What must you do to successfully run a diagnostic on the modem when you click the Query Modem button?

26. Click OK to close the Standard 56000 bps Modem Properties dialog box.

27. Click OK to close the Phone And Modem Options dialog box.

28. Close the Printers And Other Hardware window.

29. Log off the computer.

LAB REVIEW QUESTIONS

Estimated completion time: 15 minutes

1. In Exercise 7-2, would selecting the Turn On ClickLock check box on the Buttons tab of the Mouse Properties dialog box help to solve Herb's double-clicking problem? Why or why not?

2. In Exercise 7-1, when you selected a new screen resolution, you were given 15 seconds to confirm your selection before the display reverted to its previous settings. Why do the display settings behave this way?

3. Herb, the user from Exercise 7-2, calls the help desk from the road and says that after lending his laptop computer to a colleague, he got it back to find that the mouse buttons are not working properly. Double-clicking on a desktop icon opens the context menu instead of launching the program. What can he do to fix this problem?

4. In Exercise 7-3, why is the Maximum Port Speed value for the modem you installed set at 115200 when the maximum possible speed of the modem you installed is 56000 bps?

LAB CHALLENGE 7-1: ADJUSTING ICON TEXT SIZE

Estimated completion time: 30 minutes

Margaret, the user from Exercise 7-1, calls the help desk again, complaining that although she likes the "bigger desktop" you gave her by increasing the screen resolution, she is having trouble reading the small text of the desktop icons. To complete this challenge, write out the procedures for two different methods of increasing the size of the icon text on the desktop. Then perform one of the procedures and take a screen shot of the entire desktop showing the enlarged text, and paste it into a WordPad document named Computer*xx*Lab07-4.rtf (where *xx* is the number assigned to your computer by your instructor) to turn in at the end of the lab.

NTFS PERMISSIONS AND WINDOWS DESKTOP SUPPORT

Troubleshooting Lab A is a practical application of the knowledge you have acquired from Labs 1 through 7. Your instructor or lab assistant has changed your computer configuration, causing it to "break." Your task in this lab will be to apply your acquired skills to troubleshoot and resolve the break. Two scenarios are presented which lay out the parameters of the breaks and the conditions that must be met for the scenarios to be resolved. The first break scenario involves NTFS Permissions, and the second break scenario involves supporting the Windows XP desktop.

> **NOTE** In this lab, you will see the characters xx and yy. These directions assume that you are working on computers configured in pairs and that each computer has a number. When you see xx, substitute the unique number assigned to the lower-numbered computer of the pair. When you see yy, substitute the unique number assigned to the higher-numbered computer of the pair. For example, if you are using computers named Computer01 and Computer02:
>
> Computerxx = Computer01 = lower-numbered computer
>
> Computeryy = Computer02 = higher-numbered computer

> **CAUTION** **Do not proceed with this lab until you receive guidance from your instructor.** Your instructor will inform you which break scenario you will be performing (Break Scenario 1 or Break Scenario 2) and which computer to use. Your instructor or lab assistant might also have special instructions. Consult with your instructor before proceeding.

Break Scenario 1

Judy Lew, an employee at Contoso, Ltd., has just been promoted to a managerial position, replacing Max Benson, who recently left the company. Judy is taking over Max's Microsoft Windows XP computer as well, but she is having a problem.

There is a folder on the computer's C: drive called Contracts, in which Max has stored vital company documents, but Judy receives an Access Denied message whenever she tries to access it. Judy calls you at the desktop support help desk, and you go to her office to address the problem.

> **IMPORTANT**   *Perform this break scenario on Computeryy.*

> **IMPORTANT**   *For this break scenario, each user has a local user account. The password for each account is* **P@ssw0rd**.

As you resolve the problem, fill out the worksheet in the Lab Manual\TroubleshootingLabA folder and include the following information:

- A description of the problem

- A list of all steps taken to diagnose the problem, even the ones that did not work

- A description of the exact issue and solution

- A list of the tools and resources you used to help solve this problem

Break Scenario 2

Robert is a new hire at Contoso, Ltd., and on his first day at work he is assigned a desk and a computer. Robert's supervisor has provided him with the password for the computer's Administrator account, which is **P@ssw0rd**. However, when Robert logs on for the first time, no taskbar appears on the desktop. Not knowing whether he has done something wrong, Robert calls the desktop support help desk. He wants the default Windows XP taskbar to appear, and you are responsible for helping him.

> **IMPORTANT**   *Perform this break scenario on Computerxx.*

As you resolve the problem, fill out the worksheet in the Lab Manual\TroubleshootingLabA folder and include the following information:

- A description of the problem

- A list of all steps taken to diagnose the problem, even the ones that did not work

- A description of the exact issue and solution

- A list of the tools and resources you used to help solve this problem

LAB 8
SUPPORTING STORAGE DEVICES IN WINDOWS XP

This lab contains the following exercises and activities:

■ Exercise 8-1: Creating a Basic Disk Partition

■ Exercise 8-2: Extending a Basic Disk Partition

■ Exercise 8-3: Creating an Extended Partition

■ Exercise 8-4: Mounting a Volume

■ Exercise 8-5: Working with Dynamic Disks

■ Lab Review Questions

■ Lab Challenge 8-1: Creating a Striped Volume

BEFORE YOU BEGIN

To complete this lab, you must have the following information:

■ The names (Computerxx and Computeryy) assigned to your computers by your instructor

SCENARIO

You are a Microsoft Windows XP support technician for Contoso, Ltd., a company with workstations in a variety of environments. You are currently working the desktop support help desk, and you have received a number of calls this morning concerning various disk management issues.

After completing this lab, you will be able to:

■ Create basic disk partitions

■ Create dynamic disk volumes

- Convert a basic disk to a dynamic disk

- Extend volumes by using available disk space

- Mount a volume in an NTFS folder

Estimated lesson time: 80 minutes

EXERCISE 8-1: CREATING A BASIC DISK PARTITION

Estimated completion time: 15 minutes

Robert wants to store his data files separately from the operating system and application files, so when you installed Windows XP Professional Edition on his computer, you left some unallocated space on the disk for another partition. In this exercise, you create a second primary partition on Robert's computer and format it so that he can store his data files there.

1. On Computer*xx*, log on as Administrator, using the password **P@ssw0rd**.

2. Open Control Panel, and click Performance And Maintenance.

   The Performance And Maintenance window appears.

3. Click Administrative Tools.

   The Administrative Tools window appears.

4. Double-click Computer Management.

   The Computer Management console appears.

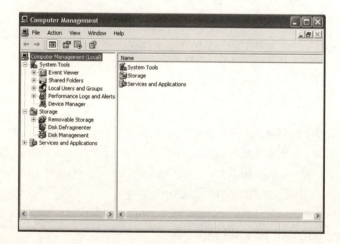

5. In the console tree, under Storage, select Disk Management.

QUESTION   How many disks are installed in the computer?

6. Copy the following table, and fill in the information for your computer in the Disk 0 column.

Disk 0
Disk Type (Basic or Dynamic)
Total Disk Size
Number of Partitions
Amount of Unallocated Space

7. In the lower half of the right pane, select the Unallocated area of Disk 0 and, on the Action menu, point to All Tasks and select New Partition.

The New Partition Wizard appears.

8. Click Next to bypass the Welcome To The New Partition Wizard page.

The Select Partition Type page appears.

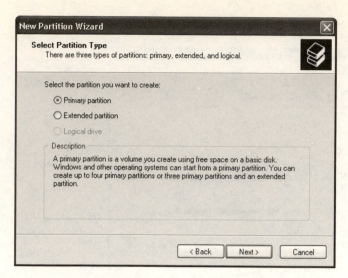

9. Leave the default Primary Partition option selected, and click Next.

The Specify Partition Size page appears.

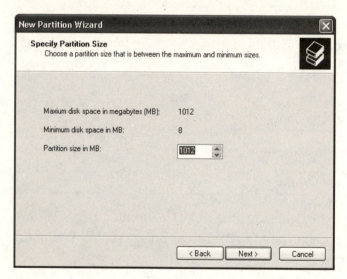

10. In the Partition Size In MB text box, type **250** and click Next.

The Assign Drive Letter Or Path page appears.

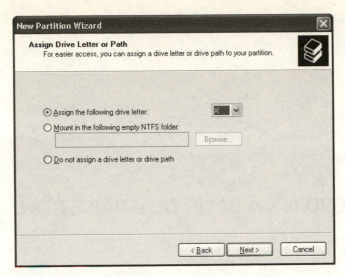

11. Leave the Assign The Following Drive Letter: option selected, and select X in the drop-down list. Then click Next.

The Format Partition page appears.

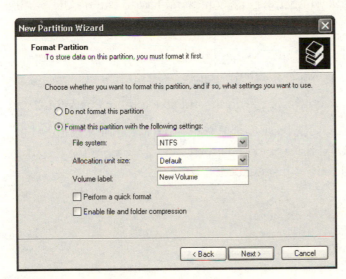

12. Leave the Format This Partition With The Following Settings: option selected, and configure the next three parameters as follows:

❑ File System: FAT32

❑ Allocation Unit Size: Default

❑ Volume Label: Data1

13. Select the Perform A Quick Format check box, and click Next.

    The Completing The New Partition Wizard page appears.

14. Click Finish.

    The new Data1 partition appears in the Disk Management snap-in.

15. Close the Administrative Tools window, but leave the Computer Management console open for future exercises.

EXERCISE 8-2: EXTENDING A BASIC DISK PARTITION

Estimated completion time: 15 minutes

Robert, the user from Exercise 8-1, is in the process of copying his data files to the partition you created for him. However, he finds that the partition is not large enough to hold all his files. To remedy the problem, you decide to extend the new partition by using some of the unallocated space left on the disk. In this exercise, you use the Diskpart.exe utility from the command line to extend the partition you created earlier.

1. On Computerxx, open Windows Explorer, expand the My Computer node, and select the X: drive letter you just created.

2. Create a new folder on the X: partition, and give it the name **WinXP**.

3. Insert your Windows XP Professional Edition installation CD into the computer's CD-ROM drive, and copy the I386 folder from the CD to the X:\WinXP folder you just created.

    QUESTION What happens?

4. Click OK.

5. Click Start, point to All Programs, point to Accessories, and click Command Prompt.

    A Command Prompt window appears.

6. In the Command Prompt window, type **diskpart** and press ENTER.

    A DISKPART> prompt appears.

NOTE   Using Diskpart.exe   If you are running Windows XP RTM or
Windows XP SP1, the Diskpart.exe version is 1.0. If you are running
Windows XP SP2, the Diskpart.exe version is 5.1.3565.

7. Type **select disk 0**, and press ENTER.

   The program responds, saying that disk 0 is now the selected disk.

8. Type **list partition**, and press ENTER.

   A list of the partitions on disk 0 appears.

   QUESTION   What is the partition number of the 250 MB partition you
   created earlier in this exercise?

9. Type **select partition #**, where # is the number of the 250 MB partition, and press ENTER.

10. Type **extend size=250**, and press ENTER.

    QUESTION   What happens?

11. Type **exit**, and press ENTER.

    The prompt reverts from DISKPART> to the standard prompt.

12. At the command prompt, type **convert x: /fs:ntfs /v /x** and press
    ENTER.

13. When the program prompts you for the volume label for drive X:, type **Data1** and press ENTER.

QUESTION   What happens?

14. Type **del x:\winxp*.* /s /q**, and press ENTER.

The files you copied to the X: partition are deleted.

15. Repeat the Convert.exe command from step 12.

QUESTION   What happens?

16. Run the Diskpart.exe program again, and repeat the commands from steps 7 through 10.

QUESTION   What is the result?

17. Type **exit**, and press ENTER to terminate the Diskpart program.

18. Close the Command Prompt window.

19. Try again to copy the I386 folder from the Windows XP Professional Edition CD to the X:\Winxp folder.

QUESTION   What is the result?

20. Close Windows Explorer, and leave the computer logged on for the next exercise.

EXERCISE 8-3: CREATING AN EXTENDED PARTITION

Estimated completion time: 10 minutes

Mary has two primary partitions on her basic disk, with some unallocated space left over. She wants you to create one more partition now, but she might want more in the future. As a result, you decide to create an extended partition out of the remaining space on the drive so that you can create as many local drives out of that space as Mary might need in the future. In this exercise, you create an extended partition and then populate it with a logical drive.

1. On Computerxx, in the Disk Management snap-in, right-click the remaining unallocated space on Disk 0 and, from the context menu, select New Partition.

   The New Partition Wizard appears.

2. Click Next on the Welcome page.

   The Select Partition Type page appears.

   QUESTION   Why is the Logical Drive option deactivated?

3. Select Extended Partition, and click Next.

   The Specify Partition Size page appears.

4. Click Next to accept the Partition Size In MB default value (which is all the available space).

   The Completing The New Partition Wizard page appears.

5. Click Finish.

   The extended partition appears in the Disk Management snap-in as Free Space.

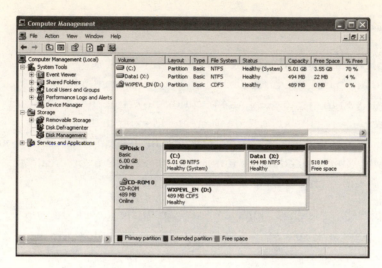

6. Right-click the Free Space segment in the Disk Management snap-in, and select New Logical Drive from the context menu.

7. In the New Partition Wizard, click Next on the Welcome page.

   The Select Partition Type page appears.

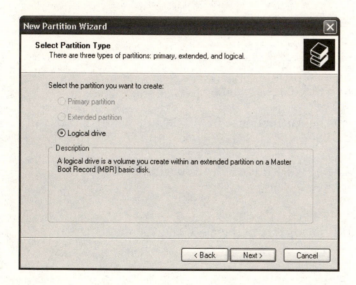

QUESTION   Why is Logical Drive the only option available on the Select Partition Type page?

8. Complete the wizard by using the following settings:

   ❑ Partition Size In MB: 250

   ❑ Assign The Following Drive Letter: Y

❑   File System: NTFS

❑   Allocation Unit Size: Default

❑   Volume Label: Data2

❑   Select the Perform A Quick Format check box.

9.   The new Data2 local drive appears in the Disk Management snap-in.

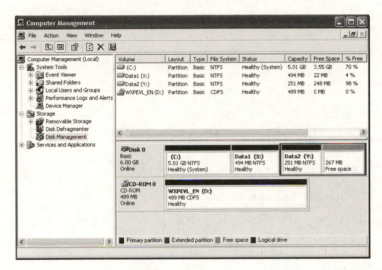

10.   Take a screen shot of the Computer Management console, showing the Disk Management snap-in and the volumes you created (by pressing ALT+PRT SCR), and paste it into a WordPad document named ComputerxxLab08-1.rtf (where *xx* is the number assigned to your computer by your instructor) to turn in at the end of the lab.

11.   Leave the Computer Management console open for the next exercise.

EXERCISE 8-4: MOUNTING A VOLUME

Estimated completion time: 10 minutes

A user named Mike calls the help desk and says that he has to copy a folder containing many large image files to his computer, but he does not have sufficient space on his C drive. Examining his computer, you notice that there is some free space left in an extended partition on the drive, so you decide to create a logical drive out of that space and mount it as a folder on the C drive. To Mike, it will appear as though the C drive gained more space.

1.   On Computerxx, open Windows Explorer and create a new folder on the computer's C drive called **Data3**.

2. In the Disk Management snap-in, right-click the remaining Free Space element on Disk 0 and, from the context menu, select New Logical Drive.

3. In the New Partition Wizard, create a logical drive using all the available space.

4. On the Assign Drive Letter Or Path page, select the Mount In The Following Empty NTFS Folder option, and in the text box, type **C:\Data3** and click Next.

5. In the Format Partition page, use the following settings and then click Next:

- ❑ File System: NTFS

- ❑ Allocation Unit Size: Default

- ❑ Volume Label: Data3

- ❑ Select the Perform A Quick Format check box.

6. Click Finish in the Completing The New Partition Wizard page to create the logical drive.

7. In Windows Explorer, select the Local Disk (C:) icon.

QUESTION   How has the icon for the Data 3 folder you created changed?

QUESTION   According to the Windows Explorer status bar, how much disk space is remaining on the C: drive?

NOTE   Displaying the Status Bar   If the status bar does not appear at the bottom of the Windows Explorer window, activate it by selecting Status Bar from the View menu.

8. Select the Data3 icon.

QUESTION   How much disk space is remaining in Data3?

9. Close Windows Explorer, but leave the Computer Management console open for the next exercise.

EXERCISE 8-5: WORKING WITH DYNAMIC DISKS

Estimated completion time: 15 minutes

Alice currently has three partitions on her basic disk: two primary partitions and one extended partition with two logical drives. She has found this arrangement to be unwieldy, and she wants to consolidate the disk into just two volumes, one of which will be part of a striped set. Unfortunately, the second hard disk drive for Alice's computer is on back order, so you cannot create the striped set yet, but you are going to prepare the system for the upgrade by converting the basic disk to a dynamic disk and consolidating the partitions. Alice has already copied all her files from the Data2 and Data3 volumes to the Data1 volume, so in this exercise, you will convert the disk to dynamic, delete the Data2 and Data3 volumes, and extend the Data1 volume to use all the remaining disk space.

1. On Computerxx, in the Disk Management snap-in, right-click the Disk 0 box in the lower half of the right pane and, from the context menu, select Convert To Dynamic Disk.

   The Convert To Dynamic Disk dialog box appears.

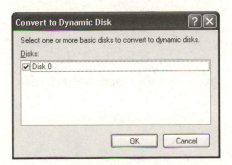

2. Leave the default Disk 0 check box selected, and click OK.

   The Disks To Convert dialog box appears.

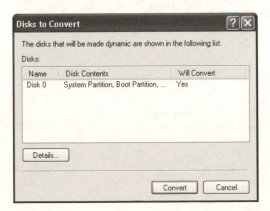

3. Click Convert.

A Disk Management message box appears, warning you that after you convert the disk to dynamic, you will not be able to start other installed operating systems from any volume on these disks.

4. Click Yes to continue.

A Convert Disk To Dynamic message box appears, warning you that the file systems on the disks to be converted must be dismounted.

5. Click Yes.

A Confirm message box appears, informing you that the computer must restart to complete the conversion.

6. Click OK.

The computer restarts.

7. After the computer restarts, log on again as Administrator and open the Disk Management snap-in, as you did in Exercise 8-1.

> **QUESTION**   What has happened to the primary partitions and the logical drives you created earlier in this lab?

8. Right-click the Data3 volume and, from the content menu, select Delete Volume.

A Delete Simple Volume dialog box appears.

9. Click Yes to confirm that you want to delete the volume.

The Data3 volume reverts to unallocated space.

10. Delete the Data2 volume in the same manner.

11. Right-click the Data1 volume and, from the context menu, select Extend Volume.

The Extend Volume Wizard appears.

12. Click Next at the Welcome To The Extend Volume Wizard page.

    The Select Disks page appears.

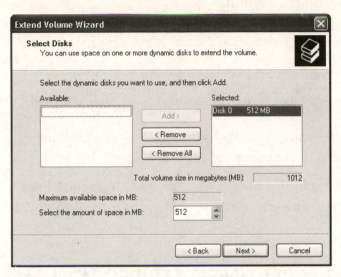

13. Click Next to accept the Select The Amount Of Space In MB default value, which is all the remaining unallocated space on the disk.

14. Click Finish in the Completing The Extend Volume Wizard page to extend the disk.

    A second Data1 volume appears in the bottom half of the Disk Management snap-in's right pane. However, only one entry for the Data1 volume appears in the list at the top of the right pane.

15. Take a screen shot of the Computer Management console, showing the Disk Management snap-in and the volumes you created (by pressing ALT+PRT SCR), and paste it into a WordPad document named ComputerxxLab08-2.rtf (where xx is the number assigned to your computer by your instructor) to turn in at the end of the lab.

16. Close the Computer Management console and the Administrative Tools window, and log off the computer.

LAB REVIEW QUESTIONS

Estimated completion time: 15 minutes

1. In Exercise 8-3, why doesn't the extended partition appear in the Disk Management snap-in's volume list at the top of the right pane?

2. In Exercise 8-4, why was it not possible to extend the C partition into the free space left on the drive, instead of mounting a volume to a folder on C?

3. In Exercise 8-5, after you converted the basic disk to a dynamic disk, how many partitions are there on the disk? How do you know?

4. If, after creating a spanned volume containing space from three hard disks, one of the hard disk drives fails, what happens to the data stored on the volume?

LAB CHALLENGE 8-1: CREATING A STRIPED VOLUME

Estimated completion time: 30 minutes

A striped volume uses space on two or more hard disks to create a single volume with greater performance capabilities than a simple or spanned volume. To complete this challenge, you must create a striped volume on a computer with two (or more) hard disks installed and unallocated space available on both drives, using the Disk Management snap-in. Make the volume as large as possible, given the amount of disk space available to you, format it using the NTFS file system, and assign it the volume label **Data4** and the drive letter Z. Write out the procedure you used to create the volume and, when you are finished, take a screen shot of the Computer Management console, showing the Disk Management snap-in and the striped volume you created (by pressing ALT+PRT SCR), and paste it into a WordPad document named Computer*xx*Lab08-3.rtf (where *xx* is the number assigned to your computer by your instructor) to turn in at the end of the lab.

LAB 9
MANAGING LOCAL AND NETWORK PRINTERS

This lab contains the following exercises and activities:

- Exercise 9-1: Installing a Printer

- Exercise 9-2: Sharing a Printer

- Exercise 9-3: Controlling Access to a Printer

- Exercise 9-4: Creating an Additional Logical Printer

- Lab Review Questions

- Lab Challenge 9-1: Creating a Printer Pool

BEFORE YOU BEGIN

To complete this lab, you must have the following:

- The names (Computer*xx* and Computer*yy*) assigned to your computers by your instructor

SCENARIO

You are a Microsoft Windows XP support technician for Contoso, Ltd., a company with workstations in a variety of environments. You have been assigned the task of installing and managing a number of new printers that the company has just received.

After completing this lab, you will be able to:

■ Install and share a printer

■ Install additional printer drivers

■ Configure advanced printer properties

■ Configure printer permissions

Estimated lesson time: 75 minutes

EXERCISE 9-1: INSTALLING A PRINTER

Estimated completion time: 15 minutes

Contoso, Ltd., has just taken delivery of several new printers that the IT director purchased through an auction. He has assigned you the task of installing the printers and making them available to the users of the company network. For the first printer, you intend to connect the unit directly to an LPT port on the computer that will function as the print server. In this exercise, you install the driver for the printer and configure it to send print jobs to the LPT2 port.

1. On Computeryy, log on to the Contoso domain as Administrator, using the password **P@ssw0rd**.

2. Click Start, and then click Printers And Faxes.

   The Printers And Faxes window appears.

3. Click the Add A Printer link.

   The Add Printer Wizard appears.

4. Click Next on the Welcome page.

   The Local Or Network Printer page appears.

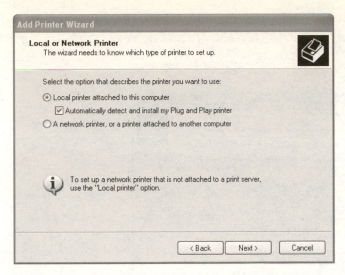

5. Leave the Local Printer Attached To This Computer option selected,
and clear the Automatically Detect And Install My Plug And Play
Printer check box. Then click Next.

> **QUESTION** Why is it necessary to clear the Automatically Detect And
> Install My Plug And Play Printer check box?

The Select A Printer Port page appears.

6. Leave the Use The Following Port option selected, and choose LPT2: (Printer Port) from the drop-down list. Then click Next.

The Install Printer Software page appears.

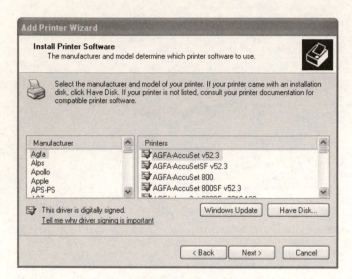

7. In the Manufacturer column, select HP, and in the Printers column, select HP LaserJet 5. Then click Next.

The Name Your Printer page appears.

8. In the Printer Name text box, type **HPLJ5** and click Next.

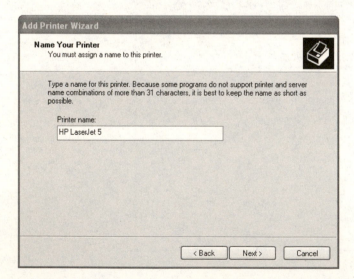

The Printer Sharing page appears.

9. Select the Do Not Share This Printer option, and then click Next

   The Print Test Page page appears.

10. Select No, and then click Next.

    The Completing The Add Printer Wizard page appears.

11. Click Finish.

    The files are copied and an icon for the HPLJ5 printer appears in the Printers And Faxes window.

12. Leave the Printers And Faxes window open and the computer logged on for the next exercise.

EXERCISE 9-2: SHARING A PRINTER

Estimated completion time: 20 minutes

With the printer installed on the computer, you are ready to make it available to network users by creating a printer share and publishing it in the Active Directory directory service database. Because the network users are running various operating systems, you must install a variety of drivers so that anyone can access the printer.

1. On Computeryy, open Windows Explorer and create a folder on the computer's C: drive called **HPLJ5**.

2. Expand the My Network Places node, and browse to the HPLJ5 share on the Server01 computer in the Contoso domain.

The \\Server01\HPLJ5 share contains Microsoft Windows 98 printer drivers for the LaserJet 5 printer you installed in Exercise 9-1.

3. Copy the entire contents of the HPLJ5 share to the C:\HPLJ5 folder you just created.

4. In the Printers And Faxes window on Computeryy, select the HPLJ5 printer icon you created in Exercise 9-1 and, from the File menu, select Properties.

The HPLJ5 Properties dialog box appears.

5. Click the Sharing tab.

6. Select the Share This Printer option, and leave the default **HPLJ5** value in the Share Name text box.

7. Ensure that List In The Directory check box is selected, and then click Additional Drivers.

The Additional Drivers dialog box appears.

NOTE *Selecting Operating Systems*   If you are running Windows XP SP2, the Additional Drivers dialog box contains an entry for the x64 version of Windows XP that does not appear in the same dialog box in Windows XP RTM and Windows XP SP1.

8. Make sure the following check boxes are selected:

   ❏ Windows 2000 Or XP

   ❏ Windows 95, 98 And Me

9. Click OK.

   A Windows 95, 98 And Me Printer Drivers dialog box appears

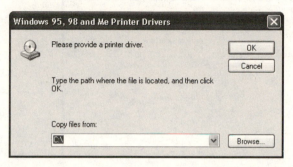

10. In the Copy Files From text box, type **C:\HPLJ5** and click OK.

   A Select Device dialog box appears.

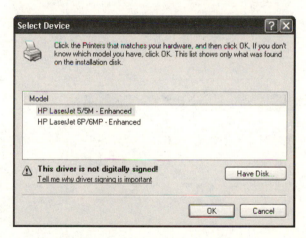

11. Select the HP LaserJet 5/5M–Enhanced model and click OK.

   QUESTION   *What happens?*

12. Take a screen shot of the Additional Drivers dialog box (by pressing ALT+PRT SCR), and paste it into a WordPad document named ComputeryyLab09-1.rtf (where *xx* is the number assigned to your computer by your instructor) to turn in at the end of the lab.

13. Click OK to close the HPLJ5 Properties dialog box.

14. Click Start and then click Search.

The Search Results window appears.

If you are using Windows XP RTM or Windows XP SP1, the window appears as follows:

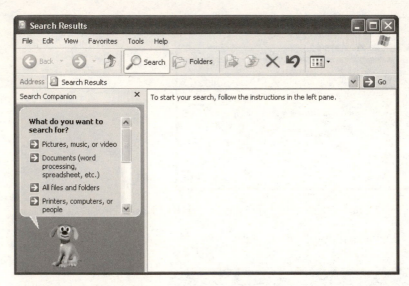

If you are running Windows XP SP2, the Search Results window is slightly different, and appears as follows:

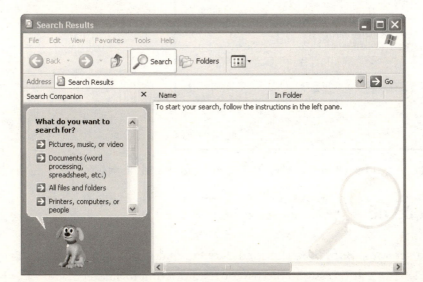

15. Click the Printers, Computers, Or People link.

16. In the What Are You Looking For? list, click the A Printer On The Network link.

The Find Printers dialog box appears.

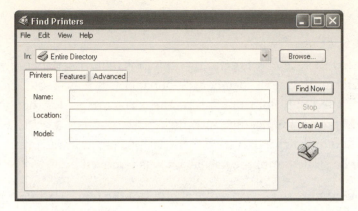

17. Click Find Now.

> **QUESTION**   What happens?

18. Leaving the Find Printers dialog box open, return to the Printers And Faxes window and open the HPLJ5 Properties dialog box again.

19. Click the Sharing tab, clear the List In The Directory check box, and click OK.

20. Return to the Find Printers dialog box, and click Find Now again.

> **QUESTION**   What happens now?

> **QUESTION**   What can you deduce from these results?

21. Open the HPLJ5 Properties dialog box again, click the Sharing tab, and select the List In The Directory check box. Then click OK.

22. Close all but the Printers And Faxes window for the next exercise.

EXERCISE 9-3: CONTROLLING ACCESS TO A PRINTER

Estimated completion time: 15 minutes

The new printer you installed has been in use for several weeks, and there have been some administrative problems you must address. First of all, from the printer's page counter and the amount of paper consumed, it is apparent that someone is using the printer to generate an enormous amount of personal work after business hours. While it is not practical to secure the printer physically, you can restrict the hours in which it can be used. In addition, you can limit who has access to the printer via permissions.

Another problem is that there are users sending print jobs requiring paper of various sizes to the printer, and when a specific type of paper is not available, the entire print queue is halted until someone inserts the correct paper for that one job. There have also been several instances in which a user's computer crashed while printing a job, and in which a user tried to interrupt a job as it was printing, causing the queue to be stalled until the partial job was removed.

In this exercise, you configure the advanced properties of the logical printer you created in Exercise 9-1 to create a more secure printing environment and to prevent these problems from occurring.

1. On Computeryy, open the HPLJ5 Properties dialog box and click the Advanced tab.

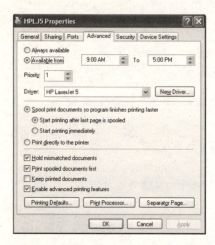

2. Select the Available From option and, in the two boxes provided, set the time that the printer is available to 9:00 AM to 5:00 PM.

> **QUESTION**   *Which of the problems described earlier will this setting help prevent, and how?*

3. Select the Start Printing After Last Page Is Spooled option.

> **QUESTION**   *Which of the problems described earlier will this setting help prevent, and how?*

4. Select the Hold Mismatched Documents check box.

> **QUESTION** *Which of the problems described earlier will this setting help prevent, and how?*

5. Click Apply, and then click the Security tab.

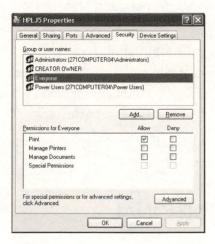

6. In the Group Or User Names list, select Everyone and then click Remove.

7. The Everyone special identity is removed from the Group Or User Names list.

8. In the same way, remove the Power Users group from the list.

9. Click Add.

The Select Users, Computers, Or Groups dialog box appears.

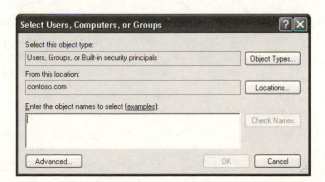

10. In the Enter The Object Names To Select (Examples) box, type **Domain Users** and click OK.

The Domain Users security principal appears in the Group Or User Names list.

11. With Domain Users highlighted, make sure that only the Print check box in the Allow column is selected.

12. Using the same procedure, add the Domain Admins group as a security principal and assign it the Print, Manage Printers, and Manage Documents permissions in the Allow column.

13. Take a screen shot of the Security tab of the HPLJ5 Properties dialog box (by pressing ALT+PRT SCR), and paste it into a WordPad document named ComputeryyLab09-2.rtf (where *yy* is the number assigned to your computer by your instructor) to turn in at the end of the lab.

14. Click OK to close the HPLJ5 Properties dialog box, and leave the Printers And Faxes window open for the next exercise.

EXERCISE 9-4: CREATING AN ADDITIONAL LOGICAL PRINTER

Estimated completion time: 10 minutes

After modifying the printer permissions and other properties in Exercise 9-3, you have found that the unauthorized use of the HPLJ5 printer has stopped. However, you received some complaints from company executives who wanted to use the printer during a late meeting with clients and were unable to do so because it was past 5:00 PM. Some of these executives were also upset because their print jobs had to wait in the queue, just like everybody else's. As a result, you must find a way to provide selected users with unlimited, priority printer access, while still limiting the access granted to the other users. In this exercise, you create a second logical printer for the same physical printer, and use it to provide additional access to the late-working executives (whom you have added to the Power Users group on the print server computer).

1. On Computeryy, in the Printers And Faxes window, create a new printer icon for the HP LaserJet 5 printer, based on the following information:

   ❑ The printer is connected to the computer's LPT2 port.

   ❑ Use the Existing HP LaserJet 5 driver.

   ❑ Assign the printer the name HPLJ5-2.

   ❑ Do not make the printer the default.

❑ Share the printer using the share name HPLJ5-2.

❑ Bypass the Location And Comment page.

❑ Do not print a test page.

2. In the Printers And Faxes window, open the HPLJ5-2 Properties dialog box and configure the additional drivers on the Sharing tab just as you did in steps 7 to 11 in Exercise 9-2.

3. Click the Advanced tab.

4. Make sure the Always Available option is selected.

5. Change the value of the Priority box from 1 to 99.

> **QUESTION**   How will modifying the Priority value help to achieve the goals stated at the beginning of this exercise?

6. Click Apply, and then click the Security tab.

7. In the Group Or User Names list, remove the Everyone security principal.

8. Modify the permissions granted to the Power Users security principal so that the group has the Print permission in the Allow column only.

> **QUESTION**   How do these permission modifications help to achieve the desired goals?

9. Click OK to close the HPLJ5-2 Properties dialog box.

10. Close the Printers And Faxes window and then log off the computer.

LAB REVIEW QUESTIONS

Estimated completion time: 15 minutes

1. In Exercise 9-2, what would be the result if you logged on to Computerxx as Administrator and attempted to search for the printer in the same way you did on Computeryy?

2. In Exercise 9-1, you didn't configure any information on the Location And Comment page as you installed the HPLJ5 printer. Based on your experiences during Exercise 9-2, how could the users of a large Active Directory network in an office building benefit if you specified the floor

number where the printer is located in the Location text box as you installed the printer?

3. In Exercise 9-2, what was the reason for installing the Windows 98 printer driver, when the computer hosting the printer is running Windows XP?

4. In Exercise 9-3, how do the changes in the permission assignments you made enhance the security of the printer installation?

LAB CHALLENGE 9-1: CREATING A PRINTER POOL

Estimated completion time: 30 minutes

As the next phase of the printer deployment at Contoso, Ltd., the IT director has allocated five identical LaserJet 5 printers to be used as a printer pool for the Order Entry department. Unlike the HPLJ5 printer, which connected to the computer using an LPT port, these five printers all have Hewlett Packard JetDirect network interface adapters in them, which have already been assigned the following IP addresses:

- 10.1.5.2
- 10.1.5.3
- 10.1.5.4
- 10.1.5.5
- 10.1.5.6

To complete this challenge, your task is to create a logical printer on your Computer*xx* and share it with the network by using the name HPLJ5 OE Pool and then configure the logical printer to function as a printer pool using the IP addresses cited earlier. Write out the procedure you used to create and configure the logical printer, take a screen shot of the Ports tab in the HPLJ5 OE Pool Properties dialog box (by pressing ALT+PRT SCR), and paste the screen shot into a WordPad document named Computer*xx*Lab09-3.rtf (where *xx* is the number assigned to your computer by your instructor) to turn in at the end of the lab.

LAB 10

SUPPORTING NETWORK CONNECTIVITY

This lab contains the following exercises and activities:

■ Exercise 10-1: Configuring the Windows TCP/IP Client Manually

■ Exercise 10-2: Testing Network Connections

■ Exercise 10-3: Installing a Network Protocol

■ Exercise 10-4: Lab Cleanup

■ Lab Review Questions

■ Lab Challenge 10-1: Using Remote Desktop

BEFORE YOU BEGIN

To complete this lab, you must have the following:

■ The names (Computerxx and Computeryy) assigned to your computers by your instructor

SCENARIO

You are a Microsoft Windows XP support technician for Contoso, Ltd., a company with workstations in a variety of environments. You have been assigned the task of building an isolated lab network using computers borrowed from the production network.

After completing this lab, you will be able to:

■ Manually configure a Windows XP TCP/IP client

■ Install a protocol module

■ Use Ping to test network connections

Estimated lesson time: 75 minutes

EXERCISE 10-1: CONFIGURING THE WINDOWS TCP/IP CLIENT MANUALLY

Estimated completion time: 15 minutes

Because the lab network you are constructing for Contoso, Ltd. is completely isolated, the computers have no access to the Dynamic Host Configuration Protocol (DHCP) servers on the production network. To prevent the Internet Protocol (IP) addresses leased by the lab network computers from expiring, you must reconfigure the Transmission Control Protocol/Internet Protocol (TCP/IP) clients to use static IP addresses and settings.

1. On Computer*xx*, log on as Administrator using the password **P@ssw0rd**.

2. Click Start, point to All Programs, point to Accessories, and click Command Prompt.

   A Command Prompt window appears.

3. In the Command Prompt window, type **ipconfig /all** and press ENTER.

4. Using the information in the Ipconfig display, complete the Computer*xx* column in the following table:

TCP/IP Parameter	Computer*xx*	Computer*yy*
IP Address		
Subnet Mask		
Default Gateway		
DNS Server		

QUESTION *From where did the computer obtain these settings? How can you tell?*

5. On Computeryy, log on to the Contoso domain as Administrator, using the password **P@ssw0rd**.

6. Repeat steps 2 through 4, and fill in the Computeryy column in the table.

7. On Computerxx, in the Command Prompt window, type **ipconfig /release** and press ENTER.

   QUESTION   What is the result of this command?

8. Click Start, and then click Control Panel.

9. Click Network And Internet Connections.

   The Network And Internet Connections window appears.

   NOTE   Using Windows XP SP2   If you are running Windows XP SP2, the Network and Internet Connections window contains several additional links that do not appear in the Windows XP RTM and Windows XP SP1 versions. However, the Network Connections link appears in both.

10. Click Network Connections.

    The Network Connections window appears.

11. Select the Local Area Connection icon, and click the Change Settings Of This Connection link.

NOTE **Opening the Local Area Connection Properties Dialog Box**
To open the Properties dialog box for a network connection, you can also click the connection icon and, from the File menu, select Properties; or you can right-click the icon and select Properties from the context menu.

The Local Area Connection Properties dialog box appears.

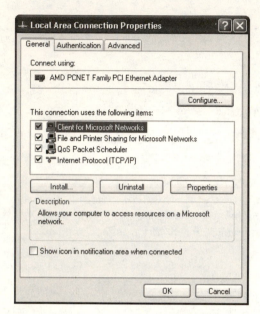

12. Select Internet Protocol (TCP/IP) in the components list, and click Properties.

The Internet Protocol (TCP/IP) Properties dialog box appears.

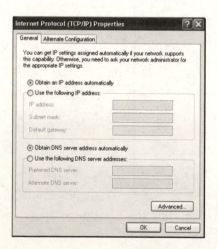

13. Select the Use The Following IP Address option.

14. In the IP Address text box, type the IP Address value from the Computer*xx* column of the table you filled out earlier in this exercise.

15. In the Subnet Mask text box, type the Subnet Mask value from the table.

16. In the Default Gateway text box, type the Default Gateway value from the table, if there is one.

17. In the Preferred DNS Server text box, type the DNS Server value from the table.

18. Take a screen shot of the Internet Protocol (TCP/IP) Properties dialog box (by pressing ALT+PRT SCR), and paste it into a WordPad document named Computer*xx*Lab10-1.rtf, where *xx* is the number assigned to your computer by your instructor, to turn in at the end of the lab.

19. Click OK to close the Internet Protocol (TCP/IP) Properties dialog box.

20. Click Close to close the Local Area Connection Properties dialog box.

21. Close the Network Connections window.

22. In the Command Prompt window, run the **ipconfig /all** command again.

> **QUESTION**   How is the Ipconfig display different from the first time you ran the ipconfig /all command?

23. Leave the Command Prompt window open for the next exercise.

EXERCISE 10-2: TESTING NETWORK CONNECTIONS

Estimated completion time: 15 minutes

After configuring the Windows XP TCP/IP client manually, you must test it by trying to connect to the other computers on the network. In this exercise, you use the Ping utility to test the computer's communications capabilities.

1. On Computer*xx*, in the Command Prompt window, type **ping 127.0.0.1** and press ENTER.

> **QUESTION**   What is the result?

> **QUESTION**   What does this result prove about Computer*xx*'s network connectivity?

2. In the Command Prompt window, type **ping server01** and press ENTER.

> **QUESTION**   What is the result?

> **QUESTION**   What does the result of this ping test prove?

> **QUESTION**   What is Server01's IP address?

> **QUESTION**   How was Computerxx able to resolve the name Server01 into its IP address?

3. In the Command Prompt window, type **ping computeryy**, where *yy* is the number assigned to the computer by your instructor, and then press ENTER.

> **QUESTION**   What was the result of the test?

> **QUESTION**   What does this result prove?

4. On Computeryy, in the Command Prompt window, use Ping to test connectivity to Computerxx.

> **QUESTION**   What is the command-line syntax you used to perform this test?

> **QUESTION**   What was the result of the test, and what does this result prove?

> **QUESTION**   Was it necessary to perform this last test? Why or why not?

5. Leave the computers logged on for the next exercise.

EXERCISE 10-3: INSTALLING A NETWORK PROTOCOL

Estimated completion time: 20 minutes

Part of the reason that you are building this lab network for Contoso, Ltd. is that the company has recently acquired a small firm and must assimilate its Novell NetWare network into Contoso's Windows network. Because some of the NetWare servers are still running the Internetwork Packet Exchange (IPX/SPX protocol suite only), you must test the PX/SPX capabilities of Windows XP. In this exercise, you install the Microsoft version of the IPX/SPX protocols on your lab computers and test their connectivity.

1. On Computerxx, open the Network Connections window and then open the Local Area Connection Properties dialog box.

> **QUESTION**   What networking software components are currently associated with the Local Area Connection interface?

2. Click Install.

The Select Network Component Type dialog box appears.

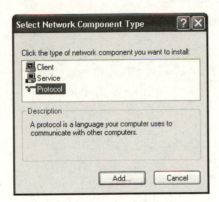

3. Select Protocol, and click Add.

The Select Network Protocol dialog box appears.

If you are running Windows XP RTM or Windows XP SP1, the Select Network Protocol dialog box appears as follows:

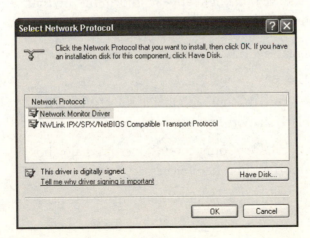

If you are running Windows XP SP2, the Select Network Protocol dialog box has an additional option, as follows:

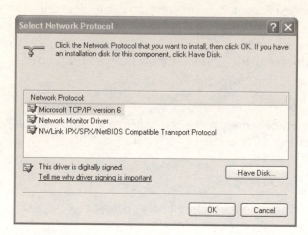

4. Select NWLink IPX/SPX/NetBIOS Compatible Transport Protocol, and click OK.

The NWLink NetBIOS and NWLink IPX/SPX/NetBIOS Compatible Transport Protocol modules are added to the components list with their check boxes selected.

5. Take a screen shot of the Local Area Connection Properties dialog box (by pressing ALT+PRT SCR), and paste it into a WordPad document named Computer*xx*Lab10-2.rtf, where *xx* is the number assigned to your computer by your instructor, to turn in at the end of the lab.

6. In the Local Area Connection Properties dialog box, clear the check box next to the Internet Protocol (TCP/IP) module.

7. Click Close to close the Local Area Connection Properties dialog box.

An Advanced Settings message box might appear, informing you that you must restart the computer.

8. If the Advanced Settings message box appears, click Yes to restart Computer*xx*.

9. On Computer*yy*, repeat steps 1 through 4 to install the NWLink IPX/SPX/NetBIOS Compatible Transport Protocol module.

10. Click Close to close the Local Area Connection Properties dialog box on Computer*yy* and restart the computer if necessary.

11. If necessary, log on to Computer*xx* as Administrator, using the password **P@ssw0rd**.

12. Open a Command Prompt window, and type **ping** plus the IP address of Computeryy, as noted in the table in Exercise 10-1. Then press ENTER.

QUESTION   What is the result?

13. In the same way, test the connection to Server01 by typing **ping 10.1.1.200** and pressing ENTER.

QUESTION   What is the result?

14. Click Start, and open the Run dialog box.

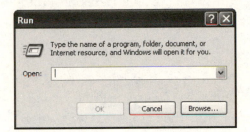

15. In the Open text box, type **\\computeryy**, where *yy* is the number assigned to the computer by your instructor, and then click OK.

QUESTION   What happens?

QUESTION   Why is it possible to access the shares on Computeryy when you are unable to ping the system?

16. In Windows Explorer, browse to the Contoso domain in My Network Places.

QUESTION   What computers are displayed in the Contoso domain? Why?

17. Close the Windows Explorer and Command Prompt windows on Computerxx, but leave the computer logged on and the Network Connections window open for the next exercise.

18. Close the Command Prompt window on Computeryy, but leave the computer logged on and the Network Connections window open for the next exercise.

EXERCISE 10-4: LAB CLEANUP

Estimated completion time: 10 minutes

1. On Computer*xx*, open the Local Area Connection Properties dialog box and select the check box next to the Internet Protocol (TCP/IP) module.

2. Open the Internet Protocol (TCP/IP) Properties dialog box, and select the Obtain An IP Address Automatically and Obtain DNS Server Address Automatically options. Then click OK.

3. Select the NWLink IPX/SPX/NetBIOS Compatible Transport Protocol module, and click Uninstall.

4. An Uninstall NWLink IPX/SPX/NetBIOS Compatible Transport Protocol message box appears, asking you to confirm your action.

5. Click Yes to uninstall the NWLink IPX/SPX/NetBIOS Compatible Transport Protocol module.

6. The NWLink IPX/SPX/NetBIOS Compatible Transport Protocol and NWLink NetBIOS modules disappear from the Local Area Connection Properties dialog box.

   A Local Network message box might appear, informing you that you must restart the computer.

7. If the Local Network message box appears, click Yes to restart the computer.

   If the Local Network message box does not appear, close the Local Area Connection Properties dialog box and the Network Connections windows and then log off the computer.

8. On Computer*yy*, use the same procedure to uninstall the NWLink IPX/SPX/NetBIOS Compatible Transport Protocol module.

9. On Computer*xx*, open a Command Prompt window, type **ping computeryy**, and then press ENTER, to test your computers' TCP/IP connectivity. If the Ping test fails, then review the steps of this exercise on both computers to ensure that they are configured properly.

LAB REVIEW QUESTIONS

Estimated completion time: 15 minutes

1. In Exercise 10-1, which of the parameters in the Internet Protocol (TCP/IP) Properties dialog box would you have to omit for Computerxx to be unable to resolve the Server01 name into its IP address.

2. In Exercise 10-2, what would be the result if you unplugged Computerxx's network cable before executing the **ping 127.0.0.1** command?

3.   In Exercise 10-3, why was it not necessary to disable the Internet Protocol (TCP/IP) module on Computeryy to demonstrate IPX connectivity?

4. In Exercise 10-3, why doesn't Server01 appear in the Contoso domain on Computerxx after you have installed and enabled the NWLink IPX/SPX/NetBIOS Compatible Transport Protocol module?

LAB CHALLENGE 10-1: USING REMOTE DESKTOP

Estimated completion time: 30 minutes

Remote Desktop enables an administrator to access a computer on the network and work directly with its interface, just as though the administrator was sitting at the remote computer's console. In this challenge, you enable Remote Desktop on your Computeryy and then use the Remote Desktop Connection client on Computerxx to connect to Computeryy. Configure the client to open a Remote Desktop window that is smaller than Computerxx's screen resolution so that you can display Computeryy's desktop as a window on Computerxx's desktop. To complete the challenge, write out the procedure you used to establish the Remote Desktop connection and then take a screen shot of the entire Computerxx desktop, containing the Remote Desktop window (by pressing PRT SCR). Paste the screen shot into a WordPad document named ComputerxxLab10-3.rtf, where xx is the number assigned to your computer by your instructor, to turn in at the end of the lab.

LAB 11
SUPPORTING INTERNET EXPLORER

This lab contains the following exercises and activities:

- Exercise 11-1: Managing Temporary Files
- Exercise 11-2: Configuring Browser Security
- Exercise 11-3: Configuring Internet Programs
- Exercise 11-4: Configuring Content Advisor
- Lab Review Questions
- Lab Challenge 11-1: Configuring Privacy Options

BEFORE YOU BEGIN

To complete this lab, you must have the following:

- The names (Computer*xx* and Computer*yy*) assigned to your computers by your instructor

SCENARIO

You are a Microsoft Windows XP support technician for Contoso, Ltd., a company with workstations in a variety of environments. You recently have been assigned a number of tasks that require you to configure (or reconfigure) the Microsoft Internet Explorer Web browser on various Windows XP computers.

After completing this lab, you will be able to:

- Configure Internet Explorer settings
- Secure Internet Explorer

Estimated lesson time: 70 minutes

EXERCISE 11-1: MANAGING TEMPORARY FILES

Estimated completion time: 10 minutes

Ralph, a salesman at Contoso, Ltd. who relies on his beloved five-year-old laptop for all his computing needs, is perpetually short on disk space because of the small drive in his computer. When he asks you to help him free up some disk space, you examine his computer and determine that a substantial portion of the drive is consumed by the temporary files created by Internet Explorer. To help Ralph keep his disk space problem under control, you decide to configure Internet Explorer to limit the amount of space it can use for temporary files.

1. On Computer*xx*, log on as Administrator, using the password **P@ssw0rd**.

2. Click Start, and then click Internet Explorer.

   The Internet Explorer window appears.

3. From the Tools menu, select Internet Options.

   The Internet Options dialog box appears with the General tab active.

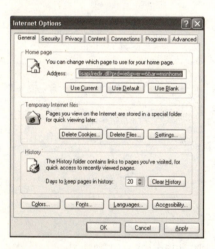

4. In the Temporary Internet Files group box, click Delete Files.

   The Delete Files dialog box appears.

5. Select the Delete All Offline Content check box, and click OK.

6. In the Temporary Internet Files group box, click Settings.

   The Settings dialog box appears.

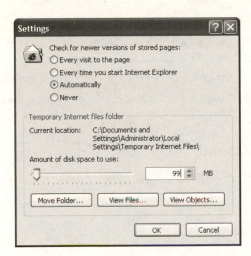

   QUESTION What is the current value of the Amount Of Disk Space To Use setting?

7. Set the Amount Of Disk Space To Use box to 50 MB, and click OK.

8. In the Internet Options dialog box, click the Advanced tab.

9. Scroll down in the Settings list and, in the Security section, select the Empty Temporary Internet Files Folder When Browser Is Closed check box. Then click OK.

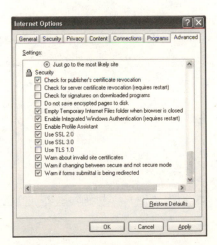

10. Close Internet Explorer, and leave the computer logged on for the next exercise.

EXERCISE 11-2: CONFIGURING BROWSER SECURITY

Estimated completion time: 25 minutes

Workers in the Order Entry department at Contoso, Ltd. use Internet Explorer to access specialized forms stored on an intranet server, but you want to prevent them from downloading the forms to their computers. This is because the forms change frequently, and it is important that everyone uses the latest version. You have been assigned the task of devising an Internet Explorer configuration that will enable the workers to access the forms but prevent them from right-clicking a link and saving the target file.

1. On Computer*xx*, open Internet Explorer.

2. In the Address box, type **http://server01** and click Go.

> **QUESTION**   *What happens?*

3. From the Tools menu, open the Internet Options dialog box.

4. On the General tab, in the Home Page group box, click Use Current to set the home page to *http://server01*.

5. Click the Security tab. Make sure that Local Intranet is selected in the Select A Web Content Zone To Specify Its Security Settings box.

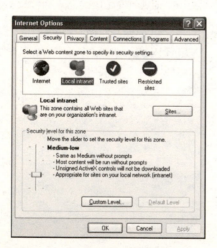

> **QUESTION**   *What is the current security level for the Local Intranet zone?*

6. Click Custom Level.

   The Security Settings dialog box appears.

7. Scroll down in the Settings list and locate the File Download setting.

   The File Download setting controls whether the user is able to save a linked file to a local drive.

   QUESTION   *What is the current value of the File Download setting?*

8. In the Reset Custom Settings section, in the Reset To drop-down list, select Medium and click Reset.

   A Warning! message box appears, asking if you want to change the security settings for the zone.

9. Click Yes.

   QUESTION   *What is the value of the File Download setting now?*

10. Reset the custom settings to High.

    QUESTION   *What is the value of the File Download setting now?*

11. Click Cancel.

12. In the Security tab, in the Security Level For This Zone section, click Default Level, then move the slider to the High position.

13. Click Apply.

14. In the Select A Web Content Zone To Specify Its Security Settings section, select Trusted Sites.

15. In the Security Level For This Zone section, make sure the default level is selected (click the Default Level button if it is available). Then click OK.

16. In Internet Explorer, click Refresh.

17. Right-click the Insurance Form link on the Contoso, Ltd. Links page, and select Save Target As from the context menu.

A Security Alert message box appears.

> **QUESTION**   Why are you unable to save the link target?

18. Click OK to clear the message box.

19. Try to save the target for the Vacation Form link in the same way.

> **QUESTION**   What is the result?

20. Open the Internet Options dialog box, and click the Security tab.

21. Select Trusted Sites, and click Sites.

The Trusted Sites dialog box appears.

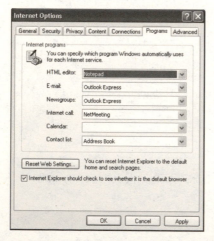

22. In the Trusted Sites dialog box, clear the Require Server Verification (Https:) For All Sites In This Zone check box.

23. In the Add This Web Site To The Zone text box, type **http://server01** and click Add.

> **QUESTION** What happens?

24. Click OK to close the Trusted Sites dialog box.

25. Click OK to close the Internet Options dialog box.

26. In Internet Explorer, click Refresh and try again to save the target for the Insurance Form link.

> **QUESTION** Why is this operation successful?

27. Try to save the target for the Vacation Form link.

> **QUESTION** Why does the operation fail?

28. Open the Trusted Sites dialog box again, and add **ftp://server01** to the list of trusted sites.

29. Take a screen shot of the Trusted Sites dialog box (by pressing ALT+ PRT SCR), and paste it into a WordPad document named ComputerxxLab11-1.rtf, where xx is the number assigned to your computer by your instructor, to turn in at the end of the lab.

30. Click OK in the Trusted Sites dialog box and in the Internet Options dialog box.

31. Refresh the Web page, and try to save the target for the Vacation Form link.

> **QUESTION** What happens?

32. Close Internet Explorer, and leave the computer logged on for the next exercise.

EXERCISE 11-3: CONFIGURING INTERNET PROGRAMS

Estimated completion time: 10 minutes

You are working the help desk at Contoso, Ltd., and you receive a call from a user who complains that when she tries to send an e-mail message from within Internet Explorer, it creates a new message using Outlook Express. However, she uses Hotmail as her e-mail software. She wants you to configure Internet Explorer so that she can create a message by using Hotmail. After talking with her for a few more minutes, you also find that she wants the following programs to be configured to work within Internet Explorer:

- HTML editor: Notepad
- E-mail client: Hotmail
- Newsgroup reader: Outlook Express
- Internet call: NetMeeting
- Contact list: Address Book

Having never configured these settings before, you open Internet Explorer on your own computer to examine them.

1. On Computer*xx*, open Internet Explorer.

2. Open the Internet Options dialog box, and click the Programs tab.

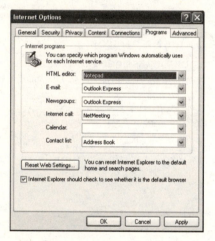

3. In the HTML Editor drop-down list, select Notepad.

4. In the E-mail drop-down list, select Hotmail.

5. Leave the Newsgroups and Internet Call drop-down lists at their default settings.

6. Click OK to close the Internet Options dialog box.

7. In Internet Explorer, on the Tools menu, point to Mail And News and click Read News.

QUESTION   What happens?

8. In Internet Explorer, click the Home button and then click the Edit With Notepad button.

QUESTION   What happens?

9. Close all the windows, and leave the computer logged on for the next exercise.

EXERCISE 11-4: CONFIGURING CONTENT ADVISOR

Estimated completion time: 15 minutes

You have been assigned the task of configuring Internet Explorer for a kiosk computer that will be used to access the Internet, primarily by teenagers. As a result, you have been told to prevent users from accessing Web sites that would generally be considered objectionable in American society. In this exercise, you use the Content Advisor in Internet Explorer to configure the browser limitations needed for this audience.

1. On Computerxx, in Internet Explorer, open the Internet Options dialog box and click the Content tab.

2. In the Content Advisor box, click Enable.

The Content Advisor dialog box appears.

3. Select the Language key, and move the slider to Level 2: Moderate Expletives.

4. Select the Nudity key, and move the slider to Level 1: Revealing Attire.

5. Select the Sex key, and move the slider to Level 1: Passionate Kissing.

6. Select the Violence key, and move the slider to Level 1: Fighting.

7. Take a screen shot of the Content Advisor dialog box (by pressing ALT+PRT SCR), and paste it into a WordPad document named Computer*xx*Lab11-2.rtf, where *xx* is the number assigned to your computer by your instructor, to turn in at the end of the lab.

8. Click the Approved Sites tab.

9. In the Allow This Web Site text box, type **http://www.microsoft.com** and click Always.

10. Click the General tab.

11. Make sure the Supervisor Can Type A Password To Allow Users To View Restricted Content check box is selected, and click Create Password.

The Create Supervisor Password dialog box appears.

12. In the Password and Confirm Password text boxes, type **P@ssw0rd** and click OK.

13. A Content Advisor message box appears, recommending that you enter a hint.

14. Click No to continue.

A Content Advisor message box appears, informing you that Internet Explorer has successfully created the supervisor password.

15. Click OK to clear the message box.

16. Click OK to close the Content Advisor dialog box

A Content Advisor message box appears, informing you that Content Advisor is enabled.

17. Click OK to clear the message box.

18. Click OK to close the Internet Options dialog box.

19. Close Internet Explorer, and log off the computer.

LAB REVIEW QUESTIONS

Estimated completion time: 10 minutes

1. In Exercise 11-1, would reducing the value of the Days To Keep Pages In History settings help the user to limit the disk space used by Internet Explorer? Why or why not?

2. In Exercise 11-2, what would happen if you failed to clear the Require Server Verification For All Sites In This Zone check box before adding *http://server01* to the list of trusted sites?

3. In Exercise 11-3, why are you unable to set the Calendar value to Microsoft Office Outlook?

LAB CHALLENGE 11-1: CONFIGURING PRIVACY OPTIONS

Estimated completion time: 30 minutes

A vice president at Contoso, Ltd. who was recently the victim of identity theft wants you to configure Internet Explorer on his computer to prevent Web sites from gathering information about him. However, the user has several Web sites that he must access and which require him to allow cookies to be stored on his computer. To accommodate the user's needs, you decide to configure Internet Explorer to block all third-party cookies and prompt the user before accepting all first-party cookies. You also plan to permit cookies from the following Internet domains:

- *contoso.com*
- *adatum.com*
- *cohovineyard.com*
- *cohowinery.com*
- *litwareinc.com*

To complete this challenge, configure the necessary Internet Explorer options to achieve the stated goals and write out a procedure for performing the configuration. Then take screen shots of the two dialog boxes that contain the settings you modified (by pressing ALT+PRT SCR), and paste them into two Wordpad documents called Computer*xx*Lab11-3.rtf and Computer*xx*Lab11-4.rtf, where *xx* is the number assigned to your computer by your instructor, to turn in at the end of the lab.

LAB 12
MONITORING SYSTEM PERFORMANCE

This lab contains the following exercises and activities:

- Exercise 12-1: Using System Monitor

- Exercise 12-2: Creating a Counter Log

- Exercise 12-3: Creating a Performance Alert

- Lab Review Questions

- Lab Challenge 12-1: Viewing a Counter Log

BEFORE YOU BEGIN

To complete this lab, you must have the following:

- The names (Computerxx and Computeryy) assigned to your computers by your instructor

SCENARIO

You are a Microsoft Windows XP support technician for Contoso, Ltd., a company with workstations in a variety of environments. You recently have been assigned a number of tasks that require you to work with the various functions of the Windows XP Performance console.

After completing this lab, you will be able to:

- **Configure a System Monitor line graph**

- **Create a baseline counter log**

- **Configure a performance alert**

Estimated lesson time: 75 minutes

EXERCISE 12-1: USING SYSTEM MONITOR

Estimated completion time: 20 minutes

The desktop support technicians at Contoso, Ltd., routinely use System Monitor in the Performance console to examine the performance levels of Windows XP workstations. However, each technician uses System Monitor in a different way. The IT director wants to create a standard set of performance counters that are easily visible in a single System Monitor line graph and that would enable the support staff to compare the performance levels of different computers. You have been given the task of selecting the performance counters for creating a standard System Monitor configuration and testing their ease of visibility on the graph.

1. Log on to Computerxx as Administrator, using the password **P@ssw0rd**.

2. Click Start, and open Control Panel.

   The Control Panel window appears. If you are running Windows XP RTM or Windows XP SP1, the window appears as follows:

If you are running Windows XP SP2, the window appears as follows:

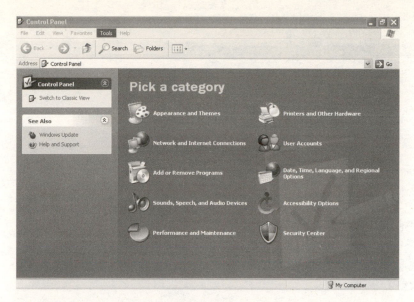

3. Click Performance And Maintenance.

The Performance And Maintenance window appears.

4. Click Administrative Tools.

5. The Administrative Tools window appears.

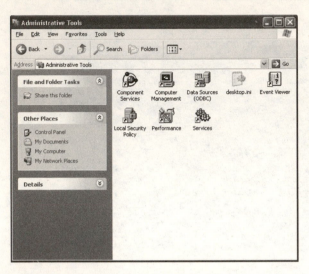

6. Double-click the Performance icon.

The Performance console appears, with the default System Monitor snap-in displayed.

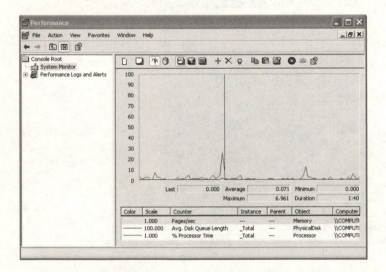

QUESTION   What counters appear in the System Monitor display by default?

7. Remove the three default counters from the System Monitor graph by selecting each one in the legend (below the line graph) and clicking the Delete button on the toolbar.

8. Click the Add button on the toolbar.

The Add Counters dialog box appears.

9. In the Performance Object drop-down list, select Server Work Queues.

10. In the Select Counters From List box, select Queue Length.

> **MORE INFO   Using Performance Counters**   For more information about the currently selected performance counter, click the Explain button.

11. In the Select Instances From List box, select 0. Then click Add.

12. Click Close to close the Add Counters dialog box.

> **QUESTION**   What happens?

> **NOTE   Understanding Counter Notation**   For each of the performance counters listed, the first term (before the colon) is the name of the performance object in which the counter is located. The second term (after the colon) is the name of the counter itself. A value in parentheses appearing after the performance object name (immediately before the colon) is the instance of the counter.

13. Using the same process, open the Add Counters dialog box and add the following counters to the graph:

❑ System: Processor Queue Length

❑ Memory: Page Faults/Sec

❑ Memory: Pages/Sec

❑ PhysicalDisk (_Total): Current Disk Queue Length

14. Click Close to close the Add Counters dialog box.

15. In the legend, select the Page Faults/Sec counter and examine the value boxes located between the legend and the graph.

> **QUESTION**   What is the maximum value for the Page Faults/Sec counter?

16. In the legend, select the Processor Queue Length counter.

> **QUESTION**   What is the maximum value for the Processor Queue Length counter?

> **QUESTION**   How is it possible for counters with such different values to be displayed effectively on the same graph?

17. Click the Properties button on the toolbar.

The System Monitor Properties dialog box appears.

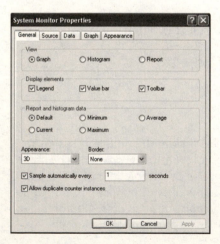

18. Click the Graph tab.

19. In the Vertical Scale group box, change the value of the Maximum field to 40 and click OK.

> **QUESTION** Does this modification make the graph easier or more difficult to read? Why?

20. Take a screen shot of the Performance console (by pressing ALT+ PRT SCR), and paste it into a WordPad document named Computer*xx*Lab12-1.rtf, where *xx* is the number assigned to your computer by your instructor, to turn in at the end of the lab.

21. From the console's Window menu, select New Window.

A new Console Root window appears in the console.

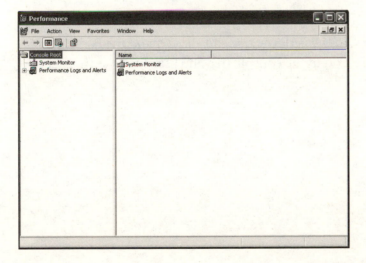

22. In the new Console Root window, click System Monitor in the scope pane and then click the Add button on the toolbar.

23. Add the following counters to the new System Monitor graph:

❑ Network Interface (select the instance for the network interface adapter in the computer): Packets/Sec

❑ Network Interface (select the instance for the network interface adapter in the computer): Output Queue Length

❑ Server: Bytes Total/Sec

24. Click Close to close the Add Counters dialog box.

> **QUESTION**   *Does this selection of counters make for an effective graph? Why or why not?*

25. Leave the Performance console open for the next exercise.

EXERCISE 12-2: CREATING A COUNTER LOG

Estimated completion time: 20 minutes

To gauge the performance level of a computer properly, it is helpful to have a baseline established under normal operating conditions that you can use to compare with levels taken under the stress of a workload. You have been given the task of taking baseline performance level readings on a new computer using the Performance console. In this exercise, you use the Performance Logs And Alerts snap-in to create a counter log for the computer, saving the baseline levels to a file for later examination.

1. On Computer*xx*, in the Performance console, expand the Performance Logs And Alerts icon in the console tree and select the Counter Logs subheading.

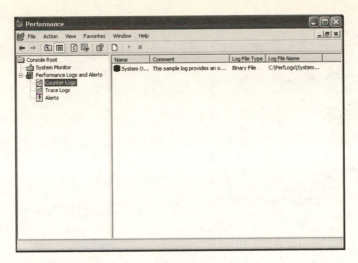

2. From the Action menu, select New Log Settings.

The New Log Settings dialog box appears.

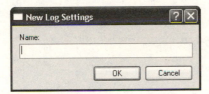

3. In the Name text box, type **Computer*xx* Baseline**, where *xx* is the number assigned to the computer, and click OK.

The Computer*xx* Baseline dialog box appears.

4. Click Add Counters.

The Add Counters dialog box appears.

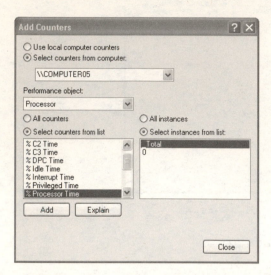

5. Using the same procedure you used to add counters to the System Monitor graph in Exercise 12-1, add the following counters:

❑ Processor (_Total): % Processor Time

❑ Processor (_Total): Interrupts/Sec

❑ System: Processor Queue Length

❑ Server Work Queues (0): Queue Length

❑ Memory: Page Faults/Sec

❑ Memory: Pages/Sec

❑ Memory: Available Bytes

❑ Memory: Committed Bytes

❑ Memory: Pool Nonpaged Bytes

❑ PhysicalDisk (_Total): Disk Bytes/Sec

❑ PhysicalDisk (_Total): Avg. Disk Bytes/Transfer

❑ PhysicalDisk (_Total): Current Disk Queue Length

❑ PhysicalDisk (_Total): % Disk Time

❑ LogicalDisk (_Total): % Free Space

❑ Network Interface (select the All Instances option): Bytes Total/Sec

❑ Network Interface (select the All Instances option): Output Queue
Length

❑ Server: Bytes Total/Sec

6. Click Close.

7. Set the Interval value to 10 and the Units value to Seconds.

8. In the Run As text box, type **Administrator**.

9. Click Set Password.

The Set Password dialog box appears.

10. Type **P@ssw0rd** in the Password and Confirm Password text boxes,
and click OK.

11. Click the Log Files tab.

12. Change the value of the End File Names With drop-down list to
yyyymmdd.

QUESTION   What will be the exact name of the counter log you are
about to create? How can you tell?

13. Click the Schedule tab.

14. In the Start Log box, select the Manually (Using The Shortcut Menu) option.

15. In the Stop Log group box, select the After option and set the interval to 5 minutes.

For the purposes of this lab exercise, you are configuring the counter log to capture data for 5 minutes. On a production server, your baseline log should run for at least several hours.

16. Click OK.

A Computer*xx* Baseline message box appears, asking whether you want to create the C:\Perflogs folder, which will be the default location for the counter log files.

17. Click Yes.

QUESTION   *What happens?*

18. Take a screen shot of the Performance console (by pressing ALT+PRT SCR), and paste it into a WordPad document named Computer*xx*Lab12-2.rtf, where *xx* is the number assigned to your computer by your instructor, to turn in at the end of the lab.

19. Select the Computer*xx* Baseline counter log you just created and, from the Action menu, click Start.

The icon for the counter log changes from red to green, indicating that the log is running.

20. Leave the Performance console open for the next exercise.

EXERCISE 12-3: CREATING A PERFORMANCE ALERT

Estimated completion time: 20 minutes

The IT director at Contoso, Ltd., is considering a network upgrade to Gigabit Ethernet that would require a significant monetary expenditure, and she wants to determine how many of the network's computers would benefit from such an upgrade. As a result, you have been instructed to configure a selected group of computers to notify you when their network traffic levels exceed a specified threshold. In this exercise, you use the Performance console to create a performance alert that monitors a computer's network traffic.

1. On Computerxx, in the Performance console, under the Performance Logs And Alerts icon, select the Alerts subheading.

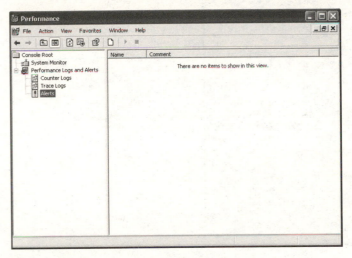

2. From the Action menu, select New Alert Settings.

The New Alert Settings dialog box appears.

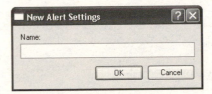

3. In the Name text box, type **Network Traffic** and click OK.

   The Network Traffic dialog box appears.

4. Click Add.

   The Add Counters dialog box appears.

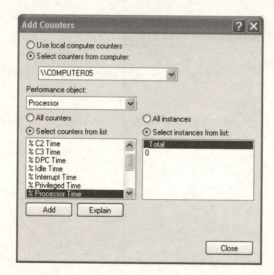

5. Add the Network Interface: Bytes Total/Sec counter and click Close.

6. Set the Alert When The Value Is drop-down list to Over and the Limit text box to 10000.

7. Set the Sample Data Every: Interval box to 30 and the Units drop-down list to Seconds.

8. In the Run As text box, type **Administrator**.

9. Click Set Password.

The Set Password dialog box appears.

10. Type **P@ssw0rd** in the Password and Confirm Password text boxes, and click OK.

11. Click the Action tab.

12. Select the Send A Network Message To check box, and type **Computeryy** in the text box, where yy is the number assigned to your other computer.

13. Click the Schedule tab.

14. In the Start Scan group box, select the Manually (Using The Shortcut Menu) option.

15. In the Stop Scan group box, set the After box to 30 and the Units drop-down list to Minutes and then click OK.

The Network Traffic alert appears in the details pane.

16. Select the Network Traffic alert you just created and, from the Action menu, choose Start.

The icon for the Network Traffic alert changes from red to green, indicating that scanning has begun.

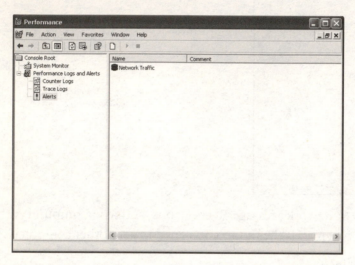

17. On Computeryy, log on to the Contoso domain as Administrator, using the password **P@ssw0rd**.

18. Open a Command Prompt window on Computeryy and, at the command prompt, type **ping computerxx −t −l 65500**, where *xx* is the number assigned to the other computer in your lab group.

19. Allow the Ping program to run for one minute.

QUESTION   What happens as a result of the Ping messages?

20. Take a screen shot of the message box (by pressing ALT+PRT SCR), and paste it into a WordPad document named ComputeryyLab12-3.rtf (where *yy* is the number assigned to your computer by your instructor) to turn in at the end of the lab.

21. On Computeryy, click OK to close the message box and, in the Command Prompt window, press CTRL+C to stop the Ping program.

22. Close the Command Prompt window.

23. On Computerxx, in the Performance console, on the Action menu, select Stop to stop the alert scanning process.

24. Close the Performance console and the Administrative Tools window.

25. Log off both computers.

LAB REVIEW QUESTIONS

Estimated completion time: 15 minutes

1. In Exercise 12-1, how would using the report view instead of the graph view affect the compatibility of the performance counters you select?

2. Under what circumstances would a counter log fail to function properly if you did not supply an account name and password in the Run As parameter?

3. In Exercise 12-3, how do the additional parameters on the Ping command line modify its functions? (Run **ping** /? for information about the program's syntax.)

4. In Exercise 12-3, what would be the result if you ran the Ping program without the −t and −l 65500 parameters?

5. In Exercise 12-4, what would happen if the Messenger service was not running on Computerxx when you tested the performance alert you created?

LAB CHALLENGE 12-1: VIEWING A COUNTER LOG

Estimated completion time: 30 minutes

In Exercise 12-2, you created a counter log for the purpose of gathering baseline performance levels for Computerxx. To complete this challenge, you must use the Performance console to display the data for the counters in the Memory performance object that you collected in the counter log file. Write out the procedure you used to display the counter log data. Then take a screen shot of the Performance console showing the counter log data (by pressing ALT+PRT SCR), and paste it into a WordPad document named ComputerxxLab12-4.rtf, where xx is the number assigned to your computer by your instructor, to turn in at the end of the lab.

TROUBLESHOOTING LAB B
SUPPORTING STORAGE DEVICES AND NETWORK CONNECTIVITY

Troubleshooting Lab B is a practical application of the knowledge you have acquired from Labs 8 through 12. Your instructor or lab assistant has changed your computer configuration, causing it to "break." Your task in this lab will be to apply your acquired skills to troubleshoot and resolve the break. Two scenarios are presented that lay out the parameters of the breaks and the conditions that must be met for the scenarios to be resolved. The first break scenario involves storage devices, and the second break scenario involves network connectivity.

> **NOTE**   In this lab, you will see the characters xx and yy. These directions assume that you are working on computers configured in pairs and that each computer has a number. When you see xx, substitute the unique number assigned to the lower-numbered computer of the pair. When you see yy, substitute the unique number assigned to the higher-numbered computer of the pair. For example, if you are using computers named Computer01 and Computer02:
>
> Computerxx = Computer01 = lower-numbered computer
>
> Computeryy = Computer02 = higher-numbered computer

> **CAUTION**   Do not proceed with this lab until you receive guidance from your instructor.   Your instructor will inform you which break scenario you will be performing (Break Scenario 1 or Break Scenario 2) and which computer to use. Your instructor or lab assistant might also have special instructions. Consult with your instructor before proceeding.

Break Scenario 1

Mary has some unallocated space on her hard disk that she wants to add to her C: drive so that she can create a folder for her music files. However, when she tried to use the Disk Management utility to expand the C: drive to include the unallocated space, she received an error message. Mary then called the help desk and asked you to fix her computer so that she could use the unallocated space for her C:\Music folder.

> **IMPORTANT** *Perform this break scenario on Computerxx.*

As you resolve the problem, fill out the worksheet in the Lab Manual\TroubleshootingLabB folder and include the following information:

- A description of the problem
- A list of all steps taken to diagnose the problem, even the ones that did not work
- A description of the exact issue and solution
- A list of the tools and resources you used to help solve this problem

Break Scenario 2

Harry, a salesman at Contoso, Ltd., has finally been given a new computer to replace the ancient model he has used for years. However, when he starts the computer for the first time, he discovers that he cannot connect to the company domain or access any network services. He calls the help desk and asks you to come over and troubleshoot his network connection.

> **IMPORTANT** *Perform this break scenario on Computeryy.*

> **IMPORTANT** *Assume that this computer must use a static TCP/IP configuration. Do not configure the computer to use DHCP.*

As you resolve the problem, fill out the worksheet in the Lab Manual\TroubleshootingLabB folder and include the following information:

- A description of the problem
- A list of all steps taken to diagnose the problem, even the ones that did not work
- A description of the exact issue and solution
- A list of the tools and resources you used to help solve this problem